D0828460

CONSTITUTIONAL
AMENDMENTS
BEYOND THE BILL OF RIGHTS

# Amendment XIV
# Due Process

# Other Books of Related Interest

**Opposing Viewpoints Series**

Civil Liberties

Feminism

Race Relations

Work

Working Women

**Current Controversies Series**

Civil Liberties

Extremist Groups

Feminism

Human Rights

CONSTITUTIONAL
AMENDMENTS
BEYOND THE BILL OF RIGHTS

# Amendment XIV
# Due Process

*Carrie Fredericks, Book Editor*

**GREENHAVEN PRESS**
*A part of Gale, Cengage Learning*

Detroit • New York • San Francisco • New Haven, Conn • Waterville, Maine • London

Christine Nasso, *Publisher*
Elizabeth Des Chenes, *Managing Editor*

© 2009 Greenhaven Press, a part of Gale, Cengage Learning.

Gale and Greenhaven Press are registered trademarks used herein under license.

*For more information, contact:*
Greenhaven Press
27500 Drake Rd.
Farmington Hills, MI 48331-3535
Or you can visit our Internet site at gale.cengage.com

For product information and technology assistance, contact us at

Gale Customer Support, 1-800-877-4253
For permission to use material from this text or product, submit all requests online at www.cengage.com/permissions

Further permissions questions can be emailed to permissionrequest@cengage.com

Articles in Greenhaven Press anthologies are often edited for length to meet page requirements. In addition, original titles of these works are changed to clearly present the main thesis and to explicitly indicate the author's opinion. Every effort is made to ensure that Greenhaven Press accurately reflects the original intent of the authors. Every effort has been made to trace the owners of copyrighted material.

Cover photograph © Tom Grill/Corbis.

**LIBRARY OF CONGRESS CATALOGING-IN-PUBLICATION DATA**

Amendment XIV : due process / Carrie Fredericks, book editor.
    p. cm. -- (Constitutional amendments: beyond the Bill of Rights)
    Includes bibliographical references and index.
    ISBN 978-0-7377-4125-4 (hardcover)
    1. Due process of law--United States--History. 2. United States. Constitution. 14th Amendment--History. 3. United States. Constitution. 12th Amendment--History--Juvenile literature. 4. Due process of law--United States. I. I. Fredericks, Carrie. II. II. Title: Amendment 14. III. III. Title: Amendment fourteen. IV. IV. Title: Due process.
    KF4765.A954 2009
    347.73'5--dc22

                               2008045077

Printed in the United States of America
1 2 3 4 5 6 7 13 12 11 10 09

**May 2009**

# Contents

## Chapter 1: Historical Background on the Fourteenth Amendment

# Chapter 2: Testing the Due Process Clause of the Fourteenth Amendment

## Chapter 3: Current Due Process Issues

# Due Process

> *"Today's Constitution is a realistic docu-
> ment of freedom only because of several
> corrective amendments. Those amend-
> ments speak to a sense of decency and
> fairness."*
>
> Thurgood Marshall

While the U.S. Constitution forms the backbone of American democracy, the amendments make the Constitution a living, ever-evolving document. Interpretation and analysis of the Constitution inform lively debate in every branch of government, as well as among students, scholars, and all other citizens, and views on various articles of the Constitution have changed over the generations. Formally altering the Constitution, however, can happen only through the amendment process. The Greenhaven Press series The Bill of Rights examines the first ten amendments to the Constitution. Constitutional Amendments: Beyond the Bill of Rights continues the exploration, addressing key amendments ratified since 1791.

The process of amending the Constitution is painstaking. While other options are available, the method used for nearly every amendment begins with a congressional bill that must pass both the Senate and the House of Representatives by a two-thirds majority. Then the amendment must be ratified by three-quarters of the states. Many amendments have been proposed since the Bill of Rights was adopted in 1791, but only seventeen have been ratified.

It may be difficult to imagine a United States where women and African Americans are prohibited from voting, where the federal government allows one human being to enslave another, or where some citizens are denied equal protection under the law. While many of our most fundamental liberties are protected by the Bill of Rights, the amendments that followed have significantly broadened and enhanced the rights of American citizens. Such rights may be taken for granted today, but when the amendments were ratified, many were considered groundbreaking and proved to be explosively controversial.

Each volume in Constitutional Amendments provides an in-depth exploration of an amendment and its impact through primary and secondary sources, both historical and contemporary. Primary sources include landmark Supreme Court rulings, speeches by prominent experts, and newspaper editorials. Secondary sources include historical analyses, law journal articles, book excerpts, and magazine articles. Each volume first presents the historical background of the amendment, creating a colorful picture of the circumstances surrounding the amendment's passage: the campaigns to sway public opinion, the congressional debates, and the struggle for ratification. Next, each volume examines the ways the court system has been used to test the validity of the amendment and addresses the ramifications of the amendment's passage. The final chapter of each volume presents viewpoints that explore current controversies and debates relating to ways in which the amendment affects our everyday lives.

Numerous features are included in each Constitutional Amendments volume:

- An originally written introduction presents a concise yet thorough overview of the amendment.

- A time line provides historical context by describing key events, organizations, and people relating to the ratification of the amendment, subsequent court cases, and the impact of the amendment.

- An annotated table of contents offers an at-a-glance summary of each primary and secondary source essay included in the volume.

- The complete text of the amendment, followed by a "plain English" explanation, brings the amendment into clear focus for students and other readers.

- Graphs, charts, tables, and maps enhance the text.

- A list of all twenty-seven Constitutional Amendments offers quick reference.

- An annotated list of court cases relevant to the amendment broadens the reader's understanding of the judiciary's role in interpreting the Constitution.

- A bibliography of books, periodicals, and Web sites aids readers in further research.

- A detailed subject index allows readers to quickly find the information they need.

With the aid of this series, students and other researchers will become better informed of their rights and responsibilities as American citizens. Constitutional Amendments: Beyond the Bill of Rights examines the roots of American democracy, bringing to life the ways the Constitution has evolved and how it has impacted this nation's history.

# Amendment Text and Explanation

## The Fourteenth Amendment to the United States Constitution

*Passed by Congress June 13, 1866. Ratified July 9, 1868.*

*Note*: Article I, Section 2, of the Constitution was modified by Section 2 of the Fourteenth Amendment.

**Section 1.**

All persons born or naturalized in the United States, and subject to the jurisdiction thereof, are citizens of the United States and of the State wherein they reside. No State shall make or enforce any law which shall abridge the privileges or immunities of citizens of the United States; nor shall any State deprive any person of life, liberty, or property, without due process of law; nor deny to any person within its jurisdiction the equal protection of the laws.

**Section 2.**

Representatives shall be apportioned among the several States according to their respective numbers, counting the whole number of persons in each State, excluding Indians not taxed. But when the right to vote at any election for the choice of electors for President and Vice-President of the United States, Representatives in Congress, the Executive and Judicial officers of a State, or the members of the Legislature thereof, is denied to any of the male inhabitants of such State, being twenty-one years of age*, and citizens of the United States, or in any way abridged, except for participation in rebellion, or other crime, the basis of representation therein shall be reduced in the proportion which the number of such male citizens shall bear to the whole number of male citizens twenty-one years of age in such State.

*Changed by Section 1 of the Twenty-sixth Amendment.*

**Section 3.**

No person shall be a Senator or Representative in Congress, or elector of President and Vice-President, or hold any office, civil or military, under the United States, or under any State, who, having previously taken an oath, as a member of Congress, or as an officer of the United States, or as a member of any State legislature, or as an executive or judicial officer of any State, to support the Constitution of the United States, shall have engaged in insurrection or rebellion against the same, or given aid or comfort to the enemies thereof. But Congress may by a vote of two-thirds of each House, remove such disability.

**Section 4.**

The validity of the public debt of the United States, authorized by law, including debts incurred for payment of pensions and bounties for services in suppressing insurrection or rebellion, shall not be questioned. But neither the United States nor any State shall assume or pay any debt or obligation incurred in aid of insurrection or rebellion against the United States, or any claim for the loss or emancipation of any slave; but all such debts, obligations and claims shall be held illegal and void.

**Section 5.**

The Congress shall have the power to enforce, by appropriate legislation, the provisions of this article.

# Explanation

## Section 1.

Section 1 is the main part of the Fourteenth Amendment dealing with citizenship, due process, privileges and immunities, and equal protection. According to Section 1, all individuals born in this country are automatically citizens of the country and the state in which they reside. Naturalized citizens are immigrants who go through the citizenship process to become naturalized citizens. There is currently great debate regarding the citizenship status of children born in the United States to illegal immigrants.

This volume deals only with Section 1, Due Process: ". . . nor shall any State deprive any person of life, liberty, or property, without due process of law . . . ." This segment of the Fourteenth Amendment guarantees that the rights of due process, guaranteed at a national level by the Fifth Amendment, are also guaranteed at the state level. Therefore, the states cannot take a person's property or infringe on his or her rights and liberties without written notification or without following a set, standard procedure that allows a citizen to have a voice in the process.

The other aspects of Section 1 deal with equal protection and privileges and immunities. The equal protection segment says that each citizen is guaranteed the same protection rights as every other citizen without fear of random prosecution by the states. The privileges and immunities segment says that states cannot enact any laws that infringe upon the privileges and immunities of any citizen.

**Section 2.**

Section 2 deals with the apportionment of representatives in Congress according to the number of residents in a particular state. The number of representatives for a state goes down if that state does not allow male citizens over the age of twenty-one to vote. The voting age was changed to eighteen by the Twenty-sixth Amendment. Women were granted the right to vote by the Nineteenth Amendment.

**Section 3.**

Section 3 says that anyone who has engaged in insurrection, rebellion, or treason cannot hold the office of senator, U.S. representative, president, vice president, or any other civil or military office. This section can be overridden by a two-thirds vote of Congress.

**Section 4.**

Section 4 addresses the public debt of the United States in the wake of the Civil War. This segment of the amendment guarantees payment owed to soldiers or citizens who fought for the Union and prevents the United States from paying for any debts incurred by Southern soldiers or slave owners.

**Section 5.**

Section 5 states that Congress has the power to make any laws necessary to enforce the provisions of the Fourteenth Amendment.

*Because the Fourteenth Amendment has many distinct provisions, no single book in this series can cover all of them. This book covers only the Due Process Clause—that is, the middle clause of Section 1.*

# Introduction

**D**ue process is the act of informing a person of a governmental action or following a standard set of practices in certain situations that allow the person to take part in the process that is occurring. There are two types of due process, procedural and substantive. Procedural due process applies mainly to governmental or court proceedings. In governmental proceedings, a citizen must be given the chance to take part in the process through a proper set of procedures, and in the case of criminal circumstances, a defendant must be given the chance to defend himself or herself against any charges through a fair trial. Substantive due process covers more individual rights, such as the right to privacy or the right to free speech. Substantive means that the government cannot take away these rights without proper justification. In both cases the government must be fair in enforcing the law, and the laws it is enforcing must also be fair.

Due process became part of the Constitution through the efforts of the state of New York. When the Continental Congress was discussing the Constitution, the New York delegation proposed that the idea of "due process for all" be part of the document. However, due process limits were discussed regarding the new Constitution. In 1787 Alexander Hamilton spoke to the New York assembly regarding the limits on due process, "The words 'due process' have a precise technical import, and are only applicable to the process and proceedings of the courts of justice; they can never be referred to an act of the legislature." According to the author and legal professor Raoul Berger in his book *Government by Judiciary; The Transformation of the Fourteenth Amendment* (1977), "No statement to the contrary will be found in any of the constitutional conventions, in the First Congress, nor in the 1866 debates."

The Fourteenth Amendment, which includes due process, became part of the Constitution following the Civil War. After the war the country struggled with the issue of rights for freed slaves, and in the years directly following the Civil War, three constitutional amendments were passed to increase the rights and privileges of former slaves. The Thirteenth Amendment, which prohibits slavery, was passed in 1865; the Fourteenth Amendment was passed by Congress in 1866 and ratified in 1868; and the Fifteenth Amendment, giving black men the right to vote, was passed in 1869 and ratified in 1870. These three amendments are often referred to as the Reconstruction amendments because the country was attempting to put itself back together after the divisiveness of the Civil War.

While most of the Fourteenth Amendment deals with congressional representation and public debt, the first section forever changed the landscape of individual rights in the United States. This section extended to all individuals involved in state actions the rights of due process and equal protection. This step was taken primarily to protect former slaves from state laws that were passed specifically to discriminate against them. In his book *Broken Promises: The Strange History of the Fourteenth Amendment*, Richard Stiller notes that democracy was slow to take root in the South in the 1860s and 1870s. After the Civil Rights Act of 1866 and the new Reconstruction acts were passed, the army patrolled cities and towns to enforce the new laws among white Southerners.

This period of rights for the freed slaves would last until 1877, when the government declared that Reconstruction was over and the U.S. Army was withdrawn from the South. This withdrawal allowed the Southern states again to discriminate against blacks, and in the years following Reconstruction, the Supreme Court heard several cases regarding the rights of blacks.

In 1876 the case *United States v. Cruikshank* came before the Court. This case involved a group of white men accused of violating the civil rights of blacks. In a unanimous decision, the Court freed the accused men. The opinion, written by Chief Justice Morrison R. Waite, stated, "The Fourteenth Amendment prohibits a State from depriving any person of life, liberty, or property, without due process of law; but this adds nothing to the rights of one citizen as against another. It simply furnishes an additional guaranty against any encroachment by the States upon the fundamental rights which belong to every citizen as a member of society." With this statement the Court said that the Fourteenth Amendment did not protect one citizen from the actions of another citizen.

In 1883 several black civil rights cases were brought to the Supreme Court and heard under one heading, *Civil Rights Cases*. By the end of the proceedings, the Supreme Court had taken away most of the rights of blacks by ruling that Congress did not have the power to protect individuals from private discrimination. The protection afforded by the Fourteenth Amendment applied only to actions by the states themselves. The majority opinion, written by Justice Joseph P. Bradley, stated, "It is State action of a particular character that is prohibited. Individual invasion of individual rights is not the subject matter of the amendment. It has a deeper and broader scope. It nullifies and makes void all State legislation, and State action of every kind, which impairs the privileges and immunities of citizens of the United States or which injures them in life, liberty or property without due process of law, or which denies to any of them the equal protection of the laws." Later, in the 1896 case *Plessy v. Ferguson*, the Supreme Court allowed racial segregation in most instances and with this decision nullified most of the rights protected by the Fourteenth Amendment.

★ In the first part of the twentieth century, due process cases became about workers' and business owners' rights. Was the right of the business owner to make a living more important than the right of the worker to make a living? These arguments were about the right to contract versus the right to fair wages. The business owners contended that they had the right to negotiate with their workers any wage contract they wanted, even if those wages were substandard. For years the Supreme Court, through case decisions, upheld this practice.

One of the best-known of these cases is *Lochner v. New York* (1905). At the turn of the century most bread was provided by small bakeries, and the bakers who were employed in these shops normally worked about 100 hours per week. In 1896 the state of New York had passed the Bakeshop Act, limiting the number of hours a baker could work to ten hours per day or sixty hours per week. Joseph Lochner, a bakery owner, was fined twice for not following this law. He eventually appealed his case to the Supreme Court, arguing that his right to contract was among the rights guaranteed by the due process clause of the Fourteenth Amendment. In 1905 the Supreme Court struck down the New York law, and in delivering the opinion of the Court, Justice Rufus W. Peckman stated, "The statute necessarily interferes with the right of contract between the employer and employees concerning the number of hours in which the latter may labor in the bakery of the employer. The general right to make a contract in relation to his business is part of the liberty of the individual protected by the Fourteenth Amendment of the Federal Constitution. Under that provision, no State can deprive any person of life, liberty or property without due process of law. The right to purchase or to sell labor is part of the liberty protected by this amendment unless there are circumstances which exclude the right."

For the next thirty years, with only some exceptions, the Supreme Court upheld the rights of business owners over the rights of workers. In 1937 this pattern began to change with the case *West Coast Hotel Co. v. Parrish*. This case upheld a Washington state minimum wage law for women and children. In giving the Court's opinion, Chief Justice Charles

Evans Hughes stated that "regulation which is reasonable in relation to its subject and is adopted in the interests of the community is due process."

In the twenty-first century, due process has taken on a new challenge. Since the September 11, 2001, attacks on the United States, the courts, the media, and Congress have been debating the issue of due process for individuals detained in the so-called war on terrorism. These debates have led to several important questions regarding due process guaranteed by the Fourteenth Amendment. Do detainees have any due process rights? Do detainees have the right to legal counsel and the use of U.S. courts even though they are not U.S. citizens? Is it a violation of due process rights to detain a terrorism suspect for an indeterminate period of time without giving any notification of the reasons for detainment? Do U.S. citizens who are detained have the right to access the U.S. court system if they are detained in another country? What is an enemy combatant, and does an enemy combatant have any due process rights?

In the last several years the Supreme Court has begun answering some of these questions. In the case *Hamdi v. Rumsfeld*, heard by the Court in 2004, the question of detaining a U.S. citizen was addressed. Yaser Esam Hamdi was captured in Afghanistan and accused of taking up arms with the Taliban, a militant Islamic movement. Hamdi asserted that he was there as a relief worker. The government wished to have Hamdi treated as an enemy combatant with no due process rights. The Court stated in its opinion, delivered by Justice Sandra Day O'Connor, "It is during our most challenging and uncertain moments that our Nation's commitment to due process is most severely tested; and it is in those times that we must preserve our commitment at home to the principles for which we fight abroad. . . . We therefore hold that a citizen-detainee seeking to challenge his classification as an enemy combatant must receive notice of the factual basis for his classification, and a fair opportunity to rebut the Government's factual assertions before a neutral decisionmaker." The Court continued, "Thus, while we do not question that our due process assessment must pay keen attention to the particular burdens faced by the Executive in the context of military action, it would turn our system of checks and balances on its head to suggest that a citizen could not make his way to court with a challenge to the factual basis for his detention by his government, simply because the Executive opposes making available such a challenge. Absent suspension of the writ by Congress, a citizen detained as an enemy combatant is entitled to this process."

In a 2004 case pertaining to foreign detainees, *Rasul v. Bush*, the petitioners claimed that they were never part of the Taliban and that they never had partaken in terrorist activities, nor were they granted the right to defend themselves against their wrongful detainment. The Court decreed that the U.S. court system had the jurisdiction to decide if detainees at Guantanamo Bay, Cuba, were rightfully detained. This decision overturned a lower court's ruling that the court system did not have the authority to decide these matters. In the majority opinion (6–3), Justice John P. Stevens concluded, "What is presently at stake is only whether the federal courts have jurisdiction to determine the legality of the Executive's potentially indefinite detention of individuals who claim to be wholly innocent of wrongdoing. Answering that question in the affirmative, we reverse the judgment of the Court of Appeals and remand for the District Court to consider in the first instance the merits of petitioners' claims." Due process cases continue to challenge the Supreme Court and will likely generate questions for years to come.

# Chronology

**1215**

The English document Magna Carta accords a free man "lawful judgment by his peers or by the law of the land."

**1354**

The English king Edward III first uses the phrase "due process of law." Later it will be determined that the Magna Carta phrase "law of the land" means "due process of law."

**1787**

At the Constitutional Convention, the proposal put forth by New York includes a provision that no person be deprived of his or her privileges, life, liberty, or property without due process of law.

**1866**

The Civil Rights Act of 1866 is passed by Congress. President Andrew Johnson vetoes this act in March, but Congress passes it again, making it law.

The Thirty-ninth Congress approves the Fourteenth Amendment, and it goes to the states for ratification. In 1866 the amendment is approved by Connecticut, New Hampshire, Tennessee, New Jersey, Oregon, and Vermont. The amendment is rejected by Texas, Georgia, North Carolina, and South Carolina.

**1867**

The Fourteenth Amendment is approved by Ohio, New York, Kansas, Pennsylvania, Illinois, West Virginia, Michigan, Minnesota, Maine, Nevada, Indiana, Missouri, Rhode Island, Wisconsin, Massachusetts, and Nebraska. The amendment is rejected by Kentucky, Virginia, Louisiana, Delaware, and Maryland.

**1868**

Ohio rescinds its approval of the Fourteenth Amendment, but the government refuses to acknowledge this action. New Jersey also rescinds its approval. The amendment is approved by Iowa, Arkansas, Florida, North Carolina, Louisiana, South Carolina, Alabama, and Georgia. Mississippi rejects the amendment. In July the Fourteenth Amendment is certified as approved by the required number of states.

**1870**

The Fifteenth Amendment is ratified. This amendment gives black men the right to vote.

**1875**

The Civil Rights Act of 1875 is passed, making any kind of segregation in public places illegal.

**1876**

In *United States v. Cruikshank*, the Supreme Court reverses the convictions of three white men found guilty of depriving two black men of life and liberty without due process of law. The original charges stemmed from the 1873 Colfax Massacre. The Court states that the Fourteenth Amendment's due process clause restricts states, not individuals.

**1883**

The Supreme Court hears what are called the Civil Rights Cases. The Court rules that the Civil Rights Act of 1875 is unconstitutional and that the government is not responsible for protecting blacks from discrimination in public places.

**1884**

The Supreme Court begins ruling that in some instances, states do not have to honor the due process clause. These rulings benefit businesses and law enforcement instead of citizens.

### 1890

The Supreme Court starts to apply substantive due process ideas to the Fourteenth Amendment in the railroad case *Chicago, Milwaukee & St. Paul Ry. C. v. Minnesota.*

### 1896

In *Plessy v. Ferguson*, the Supreme Court rules that Southern Jim Crow laws requiring the segregation of whites and blacks are constitutional. This decision completes the Supreme Court's dismantling of the Fourteenth Amendment's protection for former slaves.

### 1905

In *Lochner v. New York*, the Supreme Court decides that due process protects an individual's right to earn a living. This decision further benefits businesses instead of workers.

### 1908

In the case *Muller v. Oregon*, the Supreme Court upholds a labor-hours law for women, noting that the state has a vested interest in women's employment because of childbearing.

### 1917

In *Bunting v. Oregon*, the Supreme Court upholds another Oregon law limiting industrial workers to a ten-hour workday.

### 1920

The Supreme Court begins to use due process to protect privacy rights in the states. In the 1920s the Court rules in several cases, including *Meyer v. Nebraska* and *Pierce v. Society of Sisters*, that the due process clause protects personal liberty. In the *Pierce* case, the Court rules that according to substantive due process, parents cannot be forced to send their children to public schools.

### 1925

The Supreme Court justice Edward Sanford states that freedom of speech and of the press are liberties protected by the due process clause of the Fourteenth Amendment.

**1937**

The case *West Coast Hotel Co. v. Parrish* signals a shift in the direction of due process for individuals. The Supreme Court begins to see individual labor laws as more constitutional than the right of business owners to contract with their workers.

**1966**

In *Schmerber v. California* the Supreme Court rules that the use of police power cannot violate the Fourteenth Amendment's due process clause.

**1969**

The Court rules in *Stanley v. Georgia* that a state cannot forbid possession of obscene material, in part because of privacy rights guaranteed by the Fourteenth Amendment's due process clause. This decision will open the door to a debate on pornography and individual rights.

**1970**

In *In Re Winship*, the Supreme Court decides that due process requires criminal courts to provide proof of guilt beyond a reasonable doubt. Also, in *Goldberg v. Kelly*, the Court rules that states are required to give welfare recipients an evidentiary hearing, in addition to notification of changes in welfare payments, as part of their due process rights.

**1973**

The Supreme Court renders its opinion in the landmark abortion rights case *Roe v. Wade*. This case will spark controversy for decades to come.

**1990**

More abortion cases appear before the Supreme Court. In *Hodgson v. Minnesota*, the Court rules that a state law requiring a minor to tell both parents before receiving an abortion is unconstitutional, but that a state law allowing a minor with permission from a judge to have an abortion without parental consent is constitutional. Both decisions in this case are 5–4.

**1992**

A Pennsylvania abortion rights case, *Planned Parenthood of Southeastern Pennsylvania v. Casey*, rises to the Supreme Court, which upholds the 1973 *Roe v. Wade* decision but allows states to place new limits on abortion.

**2001**

The World Trade Center and the Pentagon are attacked on September 11. These attacks will bring into question the extent of due process rights for detainees of the new war on terrorism.

**2004**

The Supreme Court begins to address the issue of due process with detainees in the war on terrorism. In two cases, *Rasul v. Bush* and *Hamdi v. Rumsfeld*, the Court rules that detainees may have access to legal counsel to challenge their detention.

**2008**

The Supreme Court hears two new terrorism cases. One of the cases, *Munaf v. Geren*, determines that an American civilian can use American courts if he or she is being detained out of the country, and the second case, *U.S. v. Ressam*, involves the sentencing of a terrorism suspect.

# CHAPTER 1

# Historical Background on the Fourteenth Amendment

# A History of Due Process

*Morris D. Forkosch*

*In this selection Morris D. Forkosch gives an overview of the development of the idea of due process throughout history, tracing its use from ancient times up through the twentieth century. He also discusses the differences between the two types of due process, substantive and procedural. Forkosch was a professor at the University of San Diego School of Law.*

A generalized and regular procedure becomes established in man's historical and cultural life when hunters who cooperate, or the governing institutions, demand minimum standards of such procedural conduct for all. Whenever, at some point in his history, man claimed as his "due" that substance or property to which he was rightly entitled, he resorted to a procedure to obtain it which was customary, or accepted, in whatever activity he engaged. This economic, political, or cultural process, respectively, became due to persons as a right and was not necessarily the same in different nations, or even in regions or localities within a nation; regardless of what the formal or informal standards of procedure were, they were justified in some manner and continued to be claimed and variously applied as different needs arose over the years.

## The Broader Definition of "Due"

There is a second and more particularized aspect of such process that is one's due, which comes with a broadening of the meaning of "due." The term continues to mean an entitlement or right, but now has added a regularity or institutionalized formality of a legalistic nature. One reason for this addition is that a continuing basis for the civilization which characterizes all developed nations is a need for, and reliance upon, some regular form of procedure to apply the law as a means of social control. In every such country the law is usually divided and applied in both a procedural and substantive manner. The latter ordinarily deals with the content of the rules and principles which apply to those governed, while the former deals with the methods whereby the content of the law is applied in particular cases. For example, the Ten Commandments are concerned almost exclusively with substance and give the moral laws which are to be followed and obeyed, as does the Golden Rule. It appears that where a formalized belief impinges upon and determines the conduct and control of a relatively small group, detailed legalistic procedures are not urgently needed, as such religious forms dominate. But where a nation is large or controls an empire it must codify its laws and evolve uniform procedures to expedite the handling of cases, e.g., the Babylonian Code of King Hammurabi (ca. 2100? B.C.), the Roman Law of the Twelve Tables, and the English common law.

## The Ancient Idea of Due Process

Historically the idea and content of due process of law arose in very ancient times. The earliest records disclose the difficulty of the Egyptian King Harmhab in finding "two judges . . . acquainted with [the] procedure of the palace and the laws of the court." And his instructions to the judges included an admonition not to decide a case "without hearing the other" party. The oldest court record (ca. 2500 B.C.) shows that the Egyptian legal procedure included allegations of a claim, denials by the other, and the requirement that the first party produce "credible witnesses who will make oath" supporting him; otherwise the case is to be decided negatively. The earliest Mesopotamian legal records (ca. 2000 B.C.) disclose similar procedures, and the Hebraic Ninth Commandment is "Neither

*A facsimile of the Magna Carta, signed by King John of England at Runnymede. The Magna Carta laid the basis for political and personal liberty. The author believes it to be the precursor of the phrase "due process of law."© Bettmann/Corbis.*

'shalt thou bear false witness against thy neighbor." Hindu and Chinese records of the same era are hardly available, but China's reliance upon its past enables its earliest known codes to indicate procedures analogous to the preceding, and even the heterogeneous [different] and religion-oriented peoples of

India were given a monarchical [hereditary] personal form of justice which included such minimal procedures.

## Giving Notice

These minimal procedures seem to include some form of what is today called "notice" that charges are being preferred against a person, then a trial or hearing on them before a (disinterested) court which determines the matter; all these and other details are condensed into the phrase "notice and ◄ hearing." This phrase seems to entail universal standards of elementary procedural regularity and fairness. There apparently was no requirement of any degree of formality in these details, although eventually they evolved into generally adopted conventional forms. And there does not initially appear to be any general rationale to support the original necessity for these particular requirements, religious, legal, or political.

## The Beginning of Juries

[The Greek poet] Homer's description of the shield made by Hephaestus (Vulcan) for Achilles in the Trojan War depicts, in one part, the marketplace where the people "swarm" for a lawsuit; the parties each pleaded, their witnesses appeared, "The rev'rend Elders nodded o'er the Case" before they each proposed judgments, and the jury, i.e., "the partial People," then ◄ chose one proposal by acclamation and so decided the case (*The Iliad*, Book XVIII). In addition to this concept of a jury the Athenians added professional advocacy, with skill in argumentation and oratory, such as that of Demosthenes, to sway the crowds. The Roman Twelve Tables also required analogous notice and hearing, although soon a court of justice or Basilica was used for trials; eventually the Roman Emperors substituted praetors, i.e., professional judges, for the lay juries. These judicial methods were generally assimilated by the *jus gentium* which Roman tribunals applied universally, although other nations, e.g., the Celts, Gauls, and Germanic tribes, had long histories of analogous [similar] procedures. Even into the eleventh century such procedural requirements may be found, as in the decree of [the Holy Roman emperor] Conrad II in 1037 that "no man shall be deprived of a fief ... but by the laws of the empire and the judgment of his peers ..." The most famous trial in history occurred in the Praetorium at Jerusalem with notice via His [Jesus Christ's] arrest, the preferment of charges, a tribunal to hear, the giving of evidence, the opportunity to reply, and the judgment and sentencing. This idea of due process of law seems to appear early in history whenever a person was charged or accused in what is today called an "accusatorial" (criminal) or "adversary" (civil) proceeding. By contrast, the inquisitorial proceeding is applied to a person who may never even be accused but is still subjected to an inquiry and determination without knowing the charges, and who may also be compelled to give evidence which convicts him. This inquisitorial proceeding is to be differentiated from the preliminary investigatory one which may precede a criminal accusatory proceeding.

At the beginning of the modern period we find that in France the Declaration of the Rights of Man and of the Citizen (*Droits de l'homme et du citoyen*), promulgated in 1789 and made a part of the Constitution of 1793, required in Article 7 that "No man should be accused, arrested, or held in confinement, except in cases determined by the law, and according to the forms which it has prescribed." In other countries other forms and hybrids developed. The Universal Declaration of Human Rights, approved by the General Assembly of the United Nations in 1948, attempted to formulate such general principles applicable everywhere.

## The Importance of Magna Carta

For the English-speaking peoples it may be that Article 39 of Magna Carta (June 15, 1215) and its subsequent interpretation settled any doubts as to preferment of the accusatorial-adversary procedures. Its language eventually safeguarded the "free man" from being "in any way ruined . . . except by the lawful judgement of his peers or by the law of the land." In addition to this general clause the Great Charter contained other specific procedural ones although, as James Madison remarked in 1789 when proposing the future Bill of Rights, "Magna Charta does not contain any one provision for the security of those rights, respecting which the people of America are most alarmed." Magna Carta nevertheless became a sacred text in England and famous as the precursor of the phrase, "due process of law," first used by Edward III in a statute of 1354. It was, however, Sir Edward Coke's Second Institute which emphasized the concept and insisted that "law of the land" meant "due process of law"; it thus became a part of the common law and was given a natural-law interpretation and flavor.

## Due Process in Early America

The American colonial reception and modification of the idea of due process of law is disclosed in the early charters granted by the Crown, the laws of the colonists, the documents preceding and following the American Revolution, and the various state and federal constitutions. Colonial statutes and documents continued the Crown charters' general references but also became more specific. For example, acting under the grant by Charles I in 1629, the Massachusetts colonists agreed "to frame a body or grounds of laws in resemblance to a *magna charta*," and their 1641 Body of Liberties provided somewhat detailed procedures. The New England Confederation of 1643, the Dutch provisions for New Amsterdam in 1663, and the New York "Charter of Libertyes and Priviledges" of 1683, all provided for a form of due process, and due process was claimed as a right by the Congress of the Colonies held in New York in 1765. Similarly, the First Continental Congress of 1774 resolved that the colonists "are entitled to life, liberty and property ... [and] to the common law of England," and following its suggestion the colonies promulgated their own Constitutions. The famous Declaration of Rights adopted by Virginia in 1776 included the guarantee "that no man be deprived of his liberty, except by the law of the land, or the judgment of his peers," and with minor changes in language this was the general type of clause used. It was also found in the famous Northwest Ordinance of 1787.

The Constitutional Convention of 1787 discussed briefly and adopted a few procedural rights. In some of the state ratifying conventions bare majorities were obtained only because of promised amendments. Seven ratifying States appended lengthy proposals; New York's included "That no Person ought to be ... deprived of his Privileges, Franchises, Life, Liberty or Property but by due process of Law," and this may be the first use of this clause in the United States. In 1789 James Madison called the attention of the House of Representatives to these obligations and his proposals included the clause which eventually became part of the Fifth Amendment, that "No person shall ... be deprived of life, liberty, or property, without due process of law." Curiously, not a single word appears in the *Annals* [House of Representatives documents] discussing or concerning the meaning of due process of law, but it undoubtedly was not meant to include the other substantive and procedural specifics which were discussed in some detail. Of the ten amendments to the American Constitution ratified in 1791, the first eight are generally termed the Bill of Rights. The question whether these limited the federal government only, or also the states, arose in 1833. [In *Barron v. City of Baltimore*] Chief Justice [John] Marshall held in effect that they were a limitation solely on the federal government.

## Two "Due Process" Amendments

In the first important case involving the Due Process Clause it was determined that the language was "undoubtedly intended to convey the same meaning as the words 'by the law of the land,' in Magna Charta" (*Murray's Lessees v. The Hoboken Land & Improvement Co.*, 1856). This dictum limited the Clause to procedural notice and hearing, with the notice required to be adequate and the hearing fair, and subsequent opinions also followed this view (of course, "adequate" and "fair" themselves had to be interpreted, defined, and applied). Until 1868 this limitation and interpretation was not disturbed; in that year the Fourteenth Amendment was ratified, and its first section, second sentence, opens with "No State shall . . . deprive any person of," and then repeats verbatim the Fifth Amendment's language quoted above. There are thus two Due Process Clauses, the earlier one limiting the federal and the later one the state governments. Although the language is practically identical in both, their interpretation is not necessarily so; for practical purposes, however, they may be and here are treated as somewhat alike.

## Substantive Versus Procedural Due Process

The colonial and American idea of due process which now emerges, especially in the light of its English background, indicates only a procedural content. This idea is not limited to judicial or quasi-judicial proceedings. As disclosed at the outset, due process is found in many nonlegal areas such as unions, educational institutions, the church, fraternal organizations, political conventions, and various disciplinary or other proceedings. However, while due process in the nonjudicial fields in the United States has generally been restricted to procedure, in the judicial area it has been interpreted so as to include substantive rights. The basis for this is found in the separation of the Clause's language into first "life, liberty, or property," and then into "due process of law," terming them respectively substantive and procedural due process. The judiciary in effect has said that the substantive portion may stand alone as a limitation upon the governments, preventing them from depriving a person of these rights when it felt this should not occur; when permitting the deprivation, however, the Justices then insist that the procedural requirements be observed, that is, the term "without" is now activated. . . .

After the ratification of the Fourteenth Amendment the first major case to mention the new Clause was the *Slaughter-House Cases* of 1873. In his dissenting opinion Justice [Joseph P.] Bradley pointed up its usefulness, and then rejected the "great fears" that this would lead to Congressional interference "with the internal affairs of the states . . . and thus abolishing the state governments in everything but name . . ."

This judicial self-abnegation [self-denial], however, did not last long. Aroused by the 1876 *Granger Cases* which upheld a state's police power to prescribe rates charged by businesses affected with a public interest, the American bar influenced the Supreme Court to strike down "State laws, regulatory of business and industrial conditions, because they [were] unwise, improvident, or out of harmony with a particular school of thought." By 1890, with three dissenters, the Supreme Court took a decisive plunge into the substantive due process waters by requiring judicial review of a railroad commission's rate-making determination, as well as its procedure. Thus in 1927 Justice [Louis] Brandeis could write: "Despite arguments to the contrary which had seemed to me persuasive, it is well settled that the due process clause . . . applies to matters of substantive law as well as to matters of procedure." The substantive limitation may therefore be enforced against a government independently of the second requirement, that is, a government may not have any power whatever to act regardless of the excellence of its procedural methods; or, even if it has such a substantive power, it may be acting poorly in its procedural method. The consequences in each situation are different, for if a government cannot exercise a particular substantive power then it cannot act at all under it unless a judicial reversal occurs, a constitutional amendment is ratified, or another and separate power can be exercised; if, however, it is only the procedure which is bad, this may be properly corrected and the otherwise same law now upheld.

## The Power of the Court

The subsequent exercise of this power by the Supreme Court, even though in exceptional cases the federal and state governments were permitted a degree of control, produced outcries of indignation from laymen and jurists. For example, in the debate on the nomination of Chief Justice [Charles Evans] Hughes in 1930, Senator William E. Borah denounced the Court as "the economic dictator" of the country; Brandeis felt the majority was exercising "the powers of a super-legislature," while Holmes castigated their use of "no guide but" their "own discretion" so that he could "see hardly any limit but the sky to the invalidating of those [constitutional rights of the States] if they happen to strike a majority of this Court as for any reason undesirable."

The turn came with the New Deal era of 1932. The judicial retreat began with its upholding of federal and state legislation by reversing many of the earlier cases, expanding the use of the Constitution's Commerce Clause to support new laws directed against economic and social evils, and withdrawing from its due process supervisory role. However, although in 1965 it reiterated that "We do not sit as a superlegislature to determine the wisdom, need, and propriety of laws that touch economic problems, business affairs, or social conditions," the Court still retains and exercises such powers albeit their scope and depth have been voluntarily reduced and narrowed. The Justices have now transferred their major directing role from the economic to other areas, in effect becoming modern Platonic philosopher-kings in determining the minimal procedural and substantive due process of law which must be accorded all persons; nowhere else in the free nations is there such a concentration of this definitional power delegated to nine appointed individuals. These conclusions are supported by what follows.

## Current Thoughts of the Court on Due Process

In 1954 the Court's new form of activism began with the *Desegregation Case* (*Brown v. Board of Education*), which used the Fourteenth Amendment's Equal Protection Clause to strike down a state's educational segregation; simultaneously, however, the Fifth Amendment's Due Process Clause was used to denounce similar federal conduct in the District of Columbia, the Court saying "It would be unthinkable that the same Constitution would impose a lesser duty on the Federal Government." This new approach presaged an extended further broadening of the content of the Due Process Clause, and in this regard another question arose, namely, did the Barron case, mentioned above, still limit the use of the Bill of Rights only against the federal government or could it now also so limit the states? As part of their rejection of a generalized natural law content in the Due Process Clause, Justices [Hugo] Black and [William O.] Douglas urged that the specifics of the entire Bill of Rights be embraced in that Clause.

The Supreme Court has never accepted this "total incorporation" view but utilizes a selective case-by-case approach, handling each Clause in the first eight Amendments separately. The result has nevertheless been an almost total incorporation, with only a few Amendments and Clauses not so embraced.

— The Due Process Clauses thus impose limitations upon both federal and state governments in civil, criminal, and administrative proceedings, as well as upon their acting through legislative, executive, and (state) judicial branches when they "exceed" their substantive or procedural (constitutional) powers. For example, in civil matters notice continues to be vital, even though a sufficiency of (minimum) contacts enables personal jurisdiction to be obtained upon a non-resident person, and a fair hearing remains an important requirement in every type of adversary proceeding. In criminal matters a virtual revolution occurred during the 1960's. The rights of persons include not only such procedural ones but also, e.g., all of the First Amendment's substantive clauses involving free speech, religion, press, and assembly. For example, the rights to associate and also peacefully to picket and handbill within broad limits whether for labor, consumer, political, or other reasons, are protected, as are teachers and public servants protected against loyalty oaths, vague requirements, and "fishing investigations"; and education and religion are generally not intermixed.

## Due Process Defined

Due process, whether in the general area of human conduct or the particular one of law, thus connotes a procedure or method which includes regularity, fairness, equality, and a degree of justice. The idea is found in the internal disciplinary and other procedures used by labor unions, athletic organizations, social clubs, educational boards, business firms, and even religious groups, to mention but a few. The use of the term by the judiciary in the United States at first tended to follow the early procedural formulation; since the 1890's, however, a substantive content gradually broadened the meaning of due process.

# A Presidential Message

*Andrew Johnson*

*In June 1866 President Andrew Johnson sent a letter to Congress asking the members to consider adding a new amendment to the Constitution. In this letter Johnson expresses his concerns and doubts about the proposed Fourteenth Amendment, citing his objections to the process for passage and ratification. Also included in this selection is Secretary of State William H. Seward's report referring the resolution to Congress and the exact wording of the proposed amendment. Johnson was the seventeenth president of the United States, serving from 1865 to 1869.*

To the Senate and House of Representatives:

I submit to Congress a report of the Secretary of State, to whom was referred the concurrent resolution of the 18th instant, respecting a submission to the legislatures of the States of an additional article to the Constitution of the United States. It will be seen from this report that the Secretary of State had, on the 16th instant, transmitted to the governors of the several States certified copies of the joint resolution passed on the 13th instant, proposing an amendment to the Constitution.

## Concerns over the Resolution

Even in ordinary times any question of amending the Constitution must be justly regarded as of paramount importance. This importance is at the present time enhanced by the fact that the joint resolution was not submitted by the two houses for the approval of the President, and that of the thirty-six States which constitute the Union, eleven are excluded from

Andrew Johnson, "Message of the President of the United States," in U.S. Senate, 39th Congress, 1st Session, June 22, 1866.

*Andrew Johnson was the 17th president of the United States. President Johnson served from 1865 to 1869.* The Library of Congress.

representation in either House of Congress, although, with the single exception of Texas, they have been entirely restored to all their functions as States, in conformity with the organic law of the land, and have appeared at the national capital by senators and representatives who have applied for and have been refused admission to the vacant seats. Nor have the sovereign people of the nation been afforded an opportunity of expressing their views upon the important questions which the amendment involves. Grave doubts, therefore, may naturally and justly arise as to whether the action of Congress is in harmony with the sentiments of the people, and whether State legislatures, elected without reference to such an issue, should be called upon by Congress to decide respecting the ratification of the proposed amendment.

## Presidential Doubts

Waiving the question as to the constitutional validity of the proceedings of Congress upon the joint resolution proposing the amendment, or as to the merits of the article which it submits, through the executive department, to the legislatures of the States, I deem it proper to observe that the steps taken by the Secretary of State, as detailed in the accompanying report, are to be considered as purely ministerial, and in no sense whatever committing the Executive to an approval or a recommendation of the amendment to the State legislatures or to the people. On the contrary, a proper appreciation of the letter and spirit of the Constitution, as well as of the interests of national order, harmony, and union, and a due deference for an enlightened public judgment, may at this time well suggest a doubt whether any amendment to the Constitution ought to be proposed by Congress, and pressed upon the legislatures of the several States for final decision, until after the admission of such loyal senators and representatives of the now unrepresented States as have been or as may hereafter be chosen in conformity with the Constitution and laws of the United States.

ANDREW JOHNSON.

WASHINGTON, D.C., *June 22, 1866.*

# Secretary of State's Letter

Department of State,

*Washington, June 20, 1866.*

The Secretary of State, to whom was referred the concurrent resolution of the two houses of Congress of the 18th instant in the following words: "That the President of the United States be requested to transmit forthwith to the executives of the several States of the United States copies of the article of amendment proposed by Congress to the State legislatures, to amend the Constitution of the United States, passed June 13, 1866, respecting citizenship, the basis of representation, disqualification for office, and validity of the public debt of the United States, &c., to the end that the said States may proceed to act upon the said article of amendment, and that he request the executive of each State that may ratify said amendment to transmit to the Secretary of State a certified copy of such ratification," has the honor to submit the following report, namely: that on the 16th instant the Honorable Amasa Cobb, of the Committee of the House of Representatives on Enrolled Bills, brought to this department and deposited therein an enrolled resolution of the two houses of Congress, which was thereupon received by the Secretary of State and deposited among the rolls of the department, a copy of which is hereunto annexed[.] Thereupon, the Secretary of State, on the 16th instant, in conformity with the proceeding which was adopted by him in 1865 in regard to the then proposed and afterwards adopted congressional amendment of the Constitution of the United States concerning the prohibition of slavery, transmitted certified copies of the annexed resolution to the governors of the several States, together with a certificate and circular letter. A copy of both of these communications is hereunto annexed.

Respectfully submitted:

WILLIAM H. SEWARD.

The President.

## Acknowledging the Resolution

DEPARTMENT OF STATE,

> *Washington, June 16, 1866.*

SIR: I have the honor to transmit an attested copy of a resolution of Congress, proposing to the legislatures of the several States a fourteenth article to the Constitution of the United States. The decisions of the several legislatures upon the subject are required by law to be communicated to this department.

An acknowledgment of the receipt of this communication is requested by your excellency's most obedient servant,

WILLIAM H. SEWARD.

His excellency the Governor of the State of————

## A True Copy

*To all to whom these presents shall come, Greeting:*

I certify that annexed is a true copy of a concurrent resolution of Congress, entitled "Joint resolution proposing an amendment to the Constitution of the United States," the original of which resolution, received to-day, is on file in this department.

In testimony whereof, I, William H. Seward, Secretary of State of the United States, have hereunto subscribed my name and caused the seal of the Department of State to be affixed.

Done at the city of Washington, this sixteenth day of June, A.D. 1866, and of the independence of the United States of America the ninetieth.

WILLIAM H. SEWARD.

## The Resolution

[Concurrent resolution, received at Department of State June 16, 1866.]

JOINT RESOLUTION proposing an amendment to the Constitution of the United States.

*Resolved by the Senate and House of Representative of the United States of America in Congress assembled,* (two-thirds of both houses concurring,) That the following article be pro-,posed to the legislatures of the several States, as an amendment to the Constitution of the United States, which, when ratified by three-fourths of said legislatures, shall be valid as part of the Constitution, namely:

ARTICLE 14.

SECTION 1. All persons born or naturalized in the United States, and subject to the jurisdiction thereof, are citizens of the United States and of the State wherein they reside. No State shall make or enforce any law which shall abridge the privileges or immunities of citizens of the United States; nor shall any State deprive any person of life, liberty, or property without due process of law, nor deny to any person within its jurisdiction the equal protection of the laws.

SEC. 2. Representatives shall be apportioned among the several States according to their respective numbers, counting the whole number of persons in each State, excluding Indians not taxed. But when the right to vote at any election for the choice of electors for President and Vice-President of the United States, representatives in Congress, the executive and judicial officers of a State, or the members of the legislature thereof, is denied to any of the male inhabitants of such State, being twenty-one years of age and citizens of the United States, or in any way abridged, except for participation in rebellion or other crime, the basis of representation therein shall be reduced in the proportion which the number of such male citizens shall bear to the whole number of male citizens twenty-one years of age in such State.

SEC. 3. No person shall be a senator or representative in Congress, or elector of President and Vice-President, or hold any office, civil or military, under the United States, or under any State, who, having previously taken an oath as a member of Congress, or as an officer of the United States, or as a member of any State legislature, or as an executive or judicial officer of any State, to support the Constitution of the United States, shall have engaged in insurrection or rebellion against the same, or given aid or comfort to the enemies thereof. But Congress may, by a vote of two-thirds of each house, remove such disability.

Sec. 4. The validity of the public debt of the United States, authorized by law, including debts incurred for payment of pensions and bounties for services in suppressing insurrection or rebellion, shall not be questioned. But neither the United States nor any State shall assume or pay any debt or obligation incurred in aid of insurrection or rebellion against the United States, or any claim for the loss or emancipation of any slave; but all such debts, obligations, and claims shall be held illegal and void.

Sec. 5, The Congress shall have power to enforce, by appropriate legislation, the provisions of this article.

SCHUYLER COLFAX,
*Speaker of the House of Representatives.*
LA FAYETTE S. FOSTER,
*President of the Senate, pro tempore.*
Attest:
EDWD. McPHERSON, *Clerk of the House of Representatives.*
J.W. FORNEY, *Secretary of the Senate.*

# The Passage of the Fourteenth Amendment

*Eric Foner*

*In the following selection, Eric Foner discusses the background for passage of the Fourteenth Amendment. The Radical Republicans had hoped that the amendment would give rights to all men. According to Foner, the amendment fell short of what the Republicans had envisioned because it still allowed states to deny certain rights to black men. The importance of the Fourteenth Amendment in relation to the other two Reconstruction amendments is discussed, along with how all three amendments fared after ratification. Foner is the DeWitt Clinton Professor of History at Columbia University.*

On June 13, 1866, Thaddeus Stevens, the Republican floor leader in the House of Representatives and the nation's most prominent Radical Republican, rose to address his Congressional colleagues on the Fourteenth Amendment to the Constitution. Born during George Washington's administration, Stevens had enjoyed a career that embodied, as much as any other person's, the struggle against slavery and for equal rights for black Americans. In 1837, as a delegate to Pennsylvania's constitutional convention, he had refused to sign the state's new frame of government because it abrogated [abolished] African Americans' right to vote. During the Civil War, he was among the first to advocate the emancipation of the slaves and the enrollment of black soldiers. The most radical of the Radical Republicans, he even proposed confiscating the land of Confederate planters and distributing small farms to the former slaves.

## A Perfect Republic

Like other Radical Republicans, Stevens believed that Reconstruction was a golden opportunity to purge the nation of the legacy of slavery and create a "perfect republic," whose citizens enjoyed equal civil and political rights, secured by a powerful and beneficent national government. In his speech on June 13 he offered an eloquent statement of his political dream—"that the intelligent, pure and just men of this Republic ... would have so remodeled all our institutions as to have freed them from every vestige of human oppression, of inequality of rights, of the recognized degradation of the poor, and the superior caste of the rich ..." Stevens continued that the proposed amendment did not fully live up to this vision. But he offered his support. Why? "I answer, because I live among men and not among angels." A few moments later, the Fourteenth Amendment was approved by the House. It became part of the Constitution in 1868.

The Fourteenth Amendment did not fully satisfy the Radical Republicans. It did not abolish existing state governments in the South and made no mention of the right to vote for blacks. Indeed it allowed a state to deprive black men of the suffrage, so long as it suffered the penalty of a loss of representation in Congress proportionate to the black percentage of its population. (No similar penalty applied, however, when women were denied the right to vote, a provision that led many advocates of women's rights to oppose ratification of this amendment.)

## Defining Citizenship

Nonetheless, the Fourteenth Amendment was the most important constitutional change in the nation's history since the Bill of Rights. Its heart was the first section, which declared all persons born or naturalized in the United States (except Indians) to be both national and state citizens, and which prohibited the states from abridging their "privileges and im-

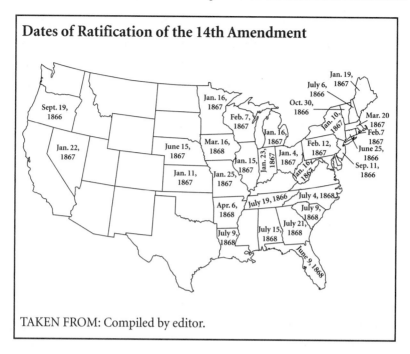

Dates of Ratification of the 14th Amendment

TAKEN FROM: Compiled by editor.

munities," depriving any person of life, liberty, or property without due process of law, or denying them "equal protection of the laws." In clothing with constitutional authority the principle of equality before the law regardless of race, enforced by the national government, this amendment permanently transformed the definition of American citizenship as well as relations between the federal government and the states, and between individual Americans and the nation. We live today in a legal and constitutional system shaped by the Fourteenth Amendment.

## The Reconstruction Amendments

The Fourteenth Amendment was one of three changes that altered the Constitution during the Civil War and Reconstruction. The Thirteenth Amendment, ratified in 1865, irrevocably abolished slavery throughout the United States. The Fifteenth, which became part of the Constitution in 1870, prohibited the states from depriving any person of the right to vote because of race (although leaving open other forms of disenfranchisement, including sex, property ownership, literacy, and payment of a poll tax). In between came the Reconstruction Act of 1867, which gave the vote to black men in the South and launched the short-lived period of Radical Reconstruction, during which, for the first time in American history, a genuine interracial democracy flourished. "Nothing in all history," wrote the abolitionist William Lloyd Garrison, equaled "this . . . transformation of four million human beings from . . . the auction-block to the ballot-box."

These laws and amendments reflected the intersection of two products of the Civil War era—a newly empowered national state and the idea of a national citizenry enjoying equality before the law. These legal changes also arose from the militant demands for equal rights from the former slaves themselves. As soon as the Civil War ended, and in some places even before, blacks gathered in mass meetings, held conventions, and drafted petitions to the federal government, demanding the same civil and political rights as white Americans. Their mobilization (given moral authority by the service of 200,000 black men in the Union army and navy in the last two years of the war) helped to place the question of black citizenship on the national agenda.

## Freedom at All Levels

The Reconstruction Amendments, and especially the Fourteenth, transformed the Constitution from a document primarily concerned with federal-state relations and the rights of property into a vehicle through which members of vulnerable minorities could stake a claim to substantive freedom and seek protection against misconduct by all levels of government. The rewriting of the Constitution promoted a sense of the document's malleability, and suggested that the rights of individual citizens were intimately connected to federal power. The Bill of Rights had linked civil liberties and the autonomy of the states. Its language—"Congress shall make no law"— reflected the belief that concentrated power was a threat to freedom. Now, rather than a threat to liberty, the federal government, declared Charles Sumner, the abolitionist Senator from Massachusetts, had become "the custodian of freedom." The Reconstruction Amendments assumed that rights required political power to enforce them. They not only authorized the federal government to override state actions that deprived citizens of equality, but each ended with a clause empowering Congress to "enforce" them with "appropriate legislation." Limiting the privileges of citizenship to white men had long been intrinsic to the practice of American democracy. Only in an unparalleled crisis could these limits have been superseded, even temporarily, by the vision of an egalitarian republic embracing black Americans as well as white and presided over by the federal government.

## Reconstruction Amendments Reflect Society

Constitutional amendments are often seen as dry documents, of interest only to specialists in legal history. In fact, as the amendments of the Civil War era reveal, they can open a window onto broad issues of political and social history. The passage of these amendments reflected the immense changes American society experienced during its greatest crisis. The amendments reveal the intersection of political debates at the top of society and the struggles of African Americans to breathe substantive life into the freedom they acquired as a result of the Civil War. Their failings—especially the fact that they failed to extend to women the same rights of citizenship afforded black men—suggest the limits of change even at a time of revolutionary transformation.

## Reconstruction Is Fleeting

Moreover, the history of these amendments underscores that rights, even when embedded in the Constitution, are not self-enforcing, and cannot be taken for granted. Reconstruction proved fragile and short-lived. Traditional ideas of racism and localism reasserted themselves, Ku Klux Klan violence disrupted the Southern Republican party, and the North retreated from the ideal of equality. Increasingly, the Supreme Court reinterpreted the Fourteenth Amendment to eviscerate its promise of equal citizenship. By the turn of the century, the Fourteenth and Fifteenth Amendments had become dead letters throughout the South. A new racial system had been put in place, resting on the disenfranchisement of black voters, segregation in every area of life, unequal education and job opportunities, and the threat of violent retribution against those who challenged the new order. The blatant violation of the Fourteenth and Fifteenth Amendments occurred with the acquiescence of the entire nation. Not until the 1950s and 1960s did a mass movement of black Southerners and white supporters, coupled with a newly activist Supreme Court, reinvigorate the Reconstruction Amendments as pillars of racial justice.

Today, in continuing controversies over abortion rights, affirmative action, the rights of homosexuals, and many other issues, the interpretation of these amendments, especially the Fourteenth, remains a focus of judicial decision-making and political debate. We have not yet created the "perfect republic" of which Stevens dreamed. But more Americans enjoy more rights and freedoms than ever before in our history.

# The "Second Constitution"

*Garrett Epps*

*The Fourteenth Amendment has often been called the "second Constitution" because of the immense changes that accompanied its passage. In the following excerpt, Garrett Epps describes how most of the rights of the Constitution stem from the Fourteenth Amendment and how the federal courts abolished many of the rights protected by this amendment after its ratification. Epps also discusses the fluidity of the Constitution and the lessons to be learned from it. Epps is a professor of law at the University of Oregon. He is the author of several fiction and nonfiction books, along with numerous magazine articles.*

Today, we live in a nation that, at least in terms of individual liberties, is one of the most democratic in history. And Americans know that they have rights. But too few understand that the source of our rights is not Philadelphia 1787 but Washington 1866. The Fourteenth Amendment has been called the "second Constitution"; in length and number of subjects touched, it is by far the most sweeping and complex change ever made in the original Constitution. Many literate Americans understand the original Framers and their world, but know virtually nothing of the second founders, or of their notions of free labor, republicanism, and equal rights. That ignorance impoverishes our public discourse—land it extends to far too many of our judges as well. Too many of them appear to believe, in the words of *The Nation* in 1866, that "the local majority is absolute," or, like [the Southern politician] John C. Calhoun, that state interests are to be given primacy over those of the nation as a whole. Too many believe that the ghost of state "sovereignty" lives on, permitting states to slow or block the national march to equality. At the dawn of a new millennium, the eminent historian David Brion Davis wrote in the *New York Times* that "the United States is only now beginning to recover from the Confederacy's ideological victory following the Civil War."

## The Influence of Federal Courts

Nowhere has that victory been more sweeping or regrettable than in the federal courts. In 1997, for example, the [William H.] Rehnquist Court invalidated an important congressional civil rights statute, the Religious Freedom Restoration Act. Relying almost entirely on segregation-era analyses of the Fourteenth Amendment, the Court held that it, not Congress, had "primary authority" for determining how to protect minority rights in the states. It dismissed John Bingham's [one of the principal authors of the Fourteenth Amendment] ideas as irrelevant to the final structure of the amendment. In 2000, the Court held that the Fourteenth Amendment did not authorize Congress to allow federal lawsuits by women victimized by gender-based violence, despite evidence of "pervasive bias" against female victims by local law enforcement authorities. "[T]he language and purpose of the Fourteenth Amendment place certain limitations on the manner in which Congress may attack discriminatory conduct," Chief Justice William H. Rehnquist wrote for the Court. "These limitations are necessary to prevent the Fourteenth Amendment from obliterating the Framers' carefully crafted balance of power between the States and the National Government"—for all the world as if the amendment had not been enacted to shift that "carefully crafted balance" sharply toward the federal side. And in 2004, the Court held that there is no constitutional problem when state legislatures deliberately redraw election districts to make sure that voters have no genuine choice of candidates—that, in other words, "the local majority" in a state can simply change the rules to ensure it will remain in power forever. "Fairness," sniffed Justice Antonin Scalia for a plurality, "does not seem to us a judicially manageable standard."

## No More Limited Federal Government

What is distressing in cases like these is not the specific result, though often it seems grievously wrong. More troubling is the failure of memory, the inability of contemporary Americans to grasp that their Constitution was changed by the second founders, that their eighteenth-century charter of limited government now contains the nineteenth-century values of equality, openness, and rule of law for all. Judges, politicians, and scholars solemnly echo [Thomas] Jefferson and [John C.] Calhoun on the role of the states. "State sovereignty" and "states' rights," ideas that by rights were buried at Gettysburg, still rule us from their graves.

## Hearing the Fourteenth Amendment

The American Constitution is not a fixed set of rules; it is an invitation to a national dialogue about concepts like due process, federalism, and equal protection. The voices of the second founders should be heard in that contemporary dialogue more clearly than they are. We can't summon their ghosts as guides, nor should we imagine that somehow we can divine their "original intent"—the intentions of the dead are and always remain one of earth's greatest mysteries. But to paraphrase Lincoln at Gettysburg, it is for us the living to dedicate ourselves to understanding and finishing the work they began. The words of the Second Constitution may not always be clear; nonetheless, they—like America itself—are a kind of prophecy, or a promise to history. Today, as in 1868, Americans often hesitate in front of claims of true equality. And yet that idea, and its corollary, a union of truly democratic states, was written in the sky by the second founders. More than a century later, it still goes before us, a cloud by day, a pillar of fire by night.

The melancholy lesson of history is that there will never come the "final triumph of the right." But it teaches another lesson as well: that prophecies and promises bear fruit over decades and centuries. We the people set out our path nearly a century and a half ago; in seasonable time, we will follow it.

# Testing the Due Process Clause of the Fourteenth Amendment

# The Due Process Clause Guarantees the Fourth Amendment Right to Privacy

*Tom C. Clark*

*In the 1961 case Mapp v. Ohio, the Supreme Court declared that the Fourteenth Amendment's due process clause reinforces the right to privacy guaranteed by the Fourth Amendment. The following article is the Supreme Court's opinion, delivered by Justice Tom C. Clark. In the opinion the Court covers search and seizure of evidence by police officers. Justice Clark also discusses the exclusionary rule and its role as part of the Fourteenth Amendment. Clark served as an associate justice of the Supreme Court from 1949 to 1967.*

M r. Justice Clark delivered the opinion of the Court.

Appellant stands convicted of knowingly having had in her possession and under her control certain lewd and lascivious books, pictures, and photographs in violation of § 2905.34 of Ohio's Revised Code. As officially stated in the syllabus to its opinion, the Supreme Court of Ohio found that her conviction was valid though "based primarily upon the introduction in evidence of lewd and lascivious books and pictures unlawfully seized during an unlawful search of defendant's home. . . ."

On May 23, 1957, three Cleveland police officers arrived at appellant's residence in that city pursuant to information that "a person [was] hiding out in the home, who was wanted for questioning in connection with a recent bombing, and that there was a large amount of policy paraphernalia being hidden in the home." Miss Mapp and her daughter by a former

"*Mapp v. Ohio* (Appeal from the Supreme Court of Ohio)," U.S. Supreme Court, 367 U.S. 643, June 19, 1961. http://supreme.justia.com.

marriage lived on the top floor of the two-family dwelling. Upon their arrival at that house, the officers knocked on the door and demanded entrance, but appellant, after telephoning her attorney, refused to admit them without a search warrant. They advised their headquarters of the situation and undertook a surveillance of the house.

The officers again sought entrance some three hours later when four or more additional officers arrived on the scene. When Miss Mapp did not come to the door immediately, at least one of the several doors to the house was forcibly opened and the policemen gained admittance. Meanwhile Miss Mapp's attorney arrived, but the officers, having secured their own entry, and continuing in their defiance of the law, would permit him neither to see Miss Mapp nor to enter the house. It appears that Miss Mapp was halfway down the stairs from the upper floor to the front door when the officers, in this high-handed manner, broke into the hall. She demanded to see the search warrant. A paper, claimed to be a warrant, was held up by one of the officers. She grabbed the "warrant" and placed it in her bosom. A struggle ensued in which the officers recovered the piece of paper and as a result of which they handcuffed appellant because she had been "belligerent" in resisting their official rescue of the "warrant" from her person. Running roughshod over appellant, a policeman "grabbed" her, "twisted [her] hand," and she "yelled [and] pleaded with him" because "it was hurting." Appellant, in handcuffs, was then forcibly taken upstairs to her bedroom where the officers searched a dresser, a chest of drawers, a closet and some suitcases. They also looked into a photo album and through personal papers belonging to the appellant. The search spread to the rest of the second floor including the child's bedroom, the living room, the kitchen and a dinette. The basement of the building and a trunk found therein were also searched. The obscene materials for possession of which she was ultimately convicted were discovered in the course of that widespread search.

*Dollree Mapp (left), a victim of an unlawful search and seizure, with her attorney A.L. Kearns. The United States Supreme Court decided that the evidence obtained in violation of the Fourteenth Amendment may not be used in criminal prosecutions.* AP Images.

At the trial, no search warrant was produced by the prosecution, nor was the failure to produce one explained or accounted for. At best, "There is, in the record, considerable doubt as to whether there ever was any warrant for the search of defendant's home." The Ohio Supreme Court believed a "reasonable argument" could be made that the conviction should be reversed "because the 'methods' employed to obtain the [evidence] . . . were such as to 'offend' a sense of justice," but the court found determinative the fact that the evidence had not been taken "from defendant's person by the use of brutal or offensive physical force against defendant."

↲ The State says that, even if the search were made without authority, or otherwise unreasonably, it is not prevented from using the unconstitutionally seized evidence at trial, citing *Wolf v. Colorado* (1949), in which this Court did indeed hold "that, in a prosecution in a State court for a State crime, the Fourteenth Amendment does not forbid the admission of evidence obtained by an unreasonable search and seizure." On this appeal, of which we have noted probable jurisdiction, it is urged once again that we review that holding.

## The Fourth and Fifth Amendments

Seventy-five years ago, in *Boyd v. United States* (1886), considering the Fourth and Fifth Amendments as running "almost into each other" on the facts before it, this Court held that the doctrines of those Amendments

> "apply to all invasions on the part of the government and its employes of the sanctity of a man's home and the privacies of life. It is not the breaking of his doors, and the rummaging of his drawers, that constitutes the essence of the offence; but it is the invasion of his indefeasible right of personal security, personal liberty and private property.... Breaking into a house and opening boxes and drawers are circumstances of aggravation; but any forcible and compulsory extortion of a man's own testimony or of his private papers to be used as evidence to convict him of crime or to forfeit his goods, is within the condemnation ... [of those Amendments]."

The Court noted that "constitutional provisions for the security of person and property should be liberally construed.... It is the duty of courts to be watchful for the constitutional rights of the citizen, and against any stealthy encroachments thereon." ...

Concluding, the Court specifically referred to the use of the evidence there seized as "unconstitutional." Less than 30 years after *Boyd*, this Court, in *Weeks v. United States* (1914), stated that:

"the Fourth Amendment ... put the courts of the United States and Federal officials, in the exercise of their power and authority, under limitations and restraints [and] ... forever secure[d] the people, their persons, houses, papers and effects against all unreasonable searches and seizures under the guise of law ... , and the duty of giving to it force and effect is obligatory upon all entrusted under our Federal system with the enforcement of the laws."

Specifically dealing with the use of the evidence unconstitutionally seized, the Court concluded[,]

"If letters and private documents can thus be seized and held and used in evidence against a citizen accused of an offense, the protection of the Fourth Amendment declaring his right to be secure against such searches and seizures is of no value, and, so far as those thus placed are concerned, might as well be stricken from the Constitution. The efforts of the courts and their officials to bring the guilty to punishment, praiseworthy as they are, are not to be aided by the sacrifice of those great principles established by years of endeavor and suffering which have resulted in their embodiment in the fundamental law of the land."

Finally, the Court in that case clearly stated that use of the seized evidence involved "a denial of the constitutional rights of the accused." Thus, in the year 1914, in the *Weeks* case, this Court "for the first time" held that, "in a federal prosecution, the Fourth Amendment barred the use of evidence secured through an illegal search and seizure." This Court has ever since required of federal law officers a strict adherence to that command which this Court has held to be a clear, specific, and constitutionally required—even if judicially implied— deterrent safeguard without insistence upon which the Fourth Amendment would have been reduced to "a form of words." It meant, quite simply, that "conviction by means of unlawful seizures and enforced confessions ... should find no sanction in the judgments of the courts . . . ," *Weeks v. United States*, and that such evidence "shall not be used at all." *Silverthorne Lumber Co. v. United States.*

## Another Aspect of the *Weeks* Case

There are in the cases of this Court some passing references to the *Weeks* rule as being one of evidence. But the plain and unequivocal language of *Weeks*—and its later paraphrase in *Wolf*—to the effect that the *Weeks* rule is of constitutional origin, remains entirely undisturbed. In *Byars v. United States* (1927), a unanimous Court declared that

> "the doctrine [cannot] . . . be tolerated *under our constitutional system*, that evidences of crime discovered by a federal officer in making a search without lawful warrant may be used against the victim of the unlawful search where a timely challenge has been interposed."

The Court, in *Olmstead v. United States* (1928), in unmistakable language restated the *Weeks* rule:

> "The striking outcome of the *Weeks* case and those which followed it was the sweeping declaration that the Fourth Amendment, although not referring to or limiting the use of evidence in courts, really forbade its introduction if obtained by government officers through a violation of the Amendment."

In *McNabb v. United States* (1943), we note this statement:

> "[A] conviction in the federal courts, the foundation of which is evidence obtained in disregard of liberties deemed fundamental by the Constitution, cannot stand. . . . And this Court has, on Constitutional grounds, set aside convictions, both in the federal and state courts, which were based upon confessions 'secured by protracted and repeated questioning of ignorant and untutored persons, in whose minds the power of officers was greatly magnified' . . . or 'who have been unlawfully held incommunicado without advice of friends or counsel.' . . ."

Significantly, in *McNabb*, the Court did then pass on to formulate a rule of evidence, saying, "[i]n the view we take of the case, however, it becomes unnecessary to reach the Constitutional issue, [for] . . . [t]he principles governing the admissibility of evidence in federal criminal trials have not been restricted . . . to those derived solely from the Constitution."

## Due Process and Privacy

In 1949, 35 years after *Weeks* was announced, this Court, in *Wolf v. Colorado*, again for the first time, discussed the effect of the Fourth Amendment upon the States through the operation of the Due Process Clause of the Fourteenth Amendment. It said: "[W]e have no hesitation in saying that, were a State affirmatively to sanction such police incursion into privacy, it would run counter to the guaranty of the Fourteenth Amendment."

Nevertheless, after declaring that the "security of one's privacy against arbitrary intrusion by the police" is "implicit in the concept of ordered liberty and, as such, enforceable against the States through the Due Process Clause," and announcing that it "stoutly adhere[d]" to the *Weeks* decision, the Court decided that the *Weeks* exclusionary rule would not then be imposed upon the States as "an essential ingredient of the right." The court's reasons for not considering essential to the right to privacy, as a curb imposed upon the States by the Due Process Clause, that which decades before had been posited as part and parcel of the Fourth Amendment's limitation upon federal encroachment of individual privacy, were bottomed on factual considerations.

While they are not basically relevant to a decision that the exclusionary rule is an essential ingredient of the Fourth Amendment as the right it embodies is vouchsafed against the States by the Due Process Clause, we will consider the current validity of the factual grounds upon which *Wolf* was based.

The Court in *Wolf* first stated that "[t]he contrariety of views of the States" on the adoption of the exclusionary rule of *Weeks* was "particularly impressive" and, in this connection, that it could not "brush aside the experience of States which deem the incidence of such conduct by the police too slight to call for a deterrent remedy ... by overriding the [States'] relevant rules of evidence."

While, in 1949, prior to the *Wolf* case, almost two-thirds of the States were opposed to the use of the exclusionary rule, now, despite the *Wolf* case, more than half of those since passing upon it, by their own legislative or judicial decision, have wholly or partly adopted or adhered to the *Weeks* rule. Significantly, among those now following the rule is California, which, according to its highest court, was "compelled to reach that conclusion because other remedies have completely failed to secure compliance with the constitutional provisions. . . ."

In connection with this California case, we note that the second basis elaborated in *Wolf* in support of its failure to enforce the exclusionary doctrine against the States was that "other means of protection" have been afforded "the right to privacy." The experience of California that such other remedies have been worthless and futile is buttressed by the experience of other States. The obvious futility of relegating the Fourth Amendment to the protection of other remedies has, moreover, been recognized by this Court since *Wolf.*

## No Fixed Formula

Likewise, time has set its face against what *Wolf* called the "weighty testimony" of *People v. Defore* (1926). There, Justice (then Judge) [Benjamin] Cardozo, rejecting adoption of the *Weeks* exclusionary rule in New York, had said that "[t]he Federal rule as it stands is either too strict or too lax." However, the force of that reasoning has been largely vitiated [debased] by later decisions of this Court. These include the recent discarding of the "silver platter" doctrine which allowed federal judicial use of evidence seized in violation of the Constitution by state agents; the relaxation of the formerly strict requirements as to standing to challenge the use of evidence thus seized, so that now the procedure of exclusion, "ultimately referable to constitutional safeguards," is available to anyone even "legitimately on [the] premises" unlawfully searched, *Jones v. United States* (1960); and, finally, the formulation of a method to prevent state use of evidence unconstitutionally seized by federal agents. Because there can be no fixed formula, we are admittedly met with "recurring questions of the reasonableness of searches," but less is not to be expected when dealing with a Constitution, and, at any rate, "[r]easonableness is in the first instance for the [trial court] . . . to determine." *United States v. Rabinowitz* (1950).

It therefore plainly appears that the factual considerations supporting the failure of the *Wolf* Court to include the *Weeks* exclusionary rule when it recognized the enforceability of the right to privacy against the States in 1949, while not basically relevant to the constitutional consideration, could not, in any analysis, now be deemed controlling.

## Search and Seizure via the Fourteenth Amendment

Some five years after *Wolf*, in answer to a plea made here Term after Term that we overturn its doctrine on applicability of the *Weeks* exclusionary rule, this Court indicated that such should not be done until the States had "adequate opportunity to adopt or reject the [*Weeks*] rule." There again, it was said: "Never until June of 1949 did this Court hold the basic search and seizure prohibition in any way applicable to the states under the Fourteenth Amendment."

And only last Term, after again carefully reexamining the *Wolf* doctrine in *Elkins v. United States, supra*, the Court pointed out that "the controlling principles" as to search and seizure and the problem of admissibility "seemed clear" until the announcement in *Wolf* "that the Due Process Clause of the Fourteenth Amendment does not itself require state courts to adopt the exclusionary rule" of the *Weeks* case. At the same time, the Court pointed out, "the underlying constitutional doctrine which *Wolf* established . . . that the Federal Constitution . . . prohibits unreasonable searches and seizures by state officers" had undermined the "foundation upon which the admissibility of state-seized evidence in a federal trial originally rested. . . ." The Court concluded that it was therefore obliged to hold, although it chose the narrower ground on which to do so, that all evidence obtained by an unconstitutional search and seizure was inadmissible in a federal court regardless of its source. Today we once again examine *Wolf*'s constitutional documentation of the right to privacy free from unreasonable state intrusion, and, after its dozen years on our books, are led by it to close the only courtroom door remaining open to evidence secured by official lawlessness in flagrant abuse of that basic right, reserved to all persons as a specific guarantee against that very same unlawful conduct. We hold that all evidence obtained by searches and seizures in violation of the Constitution is, by that same authority, inadmissible in a state court.

## Fourth Amendment Is Enforceable

Since the Fourth Amendment's right of privacy has been declared enforceable against the States through the Due Process Clause of the Fourteenth, it is enforceable against them by the same sanction of exclusion as is used against the Federal Government. Were it otherwise, then, just as without the *Weeks* rule the assurance against unreasonable federal searches and seizures would be "a form of words," valueless and undeserving of mention in a perpetual charter of inestimable human liberties, so too, without that rule, the freedom from state invasions of privacy would be so ephemeral and so neatly severed from its conceptual nexus with the freedom from all brutish means of coercing evidence as not to merit this Court's high regard as a freedom "implicit in the concept of ordered liberty." At the time that the Court held in *Wolf* that the Amendment was applicable to the States through the Due Process Clause, the cases of this Court, as we have seen, had steadfastly held that as to federal officers the Fourth Amendment included the exclusion of the evidence seized in violation of its provisions. Even *Wolf* "stoutly adhered" to that proposition. The right to privacy, when conceded operatively enforceable against the States, was not susceptible of destruction by avulsion of the sanction upon which its protection and enjoyment had always been deemed dependent under the *Boyd, Weeks* and *Silverthorne* cases. Therefore, in extending the substantive protections of due process to all constitutionally unreasonable searches—state or federal—it was logically and constitutionally necessary that the exclusion doctrine—an essential part of the right to privacy—be also insisted upon as an essential ingredient of the right newly recognized by the *Wolf* case. In short, the admission of the new constitutional right by *Wolf* could not consistently tolerate denial of its most important constitutional privilege, namely, the exclusion of the evidence which an accused had been forced to give by reason of the unlawful seizure. To hold otherwise is to grant the right but, in reality, to withhold its privilege and enjoyment. Only last year [1960], the Court itself recognized that the purpose of the exclusionary rule "is to deter—to compel respect for the constitutional guaranty in the only effectively available way—by removing the incentive to disregard it."

Indeed, we are aware of no restraint, similar to that rejected today, conditioning the enforcement of any other basic constitutional right. The right to privacy, no less important than any other right carefully and particularly reserved to the people, would stand in marked contrast to all other rights declared as "basic to a free society." This Court has not hesitated to enforce as strictly against the States as it does against the

Federal Government the rights of free speech and of a free press, the rights to notice and to a fair, public trial, including, as it does, the right not to be convicted by use of a coerced confession, however logically relevant it be, and without regard to its reliability. And nothing could be more certain than that, when a coerced confession is involved, "the relevant rules of evidence" are overridden without regard to "the incidence of such conduct by the police," slight or frequent. Why should not the same rule apply to what is tantamount to coerced testimony by way of unconstitutional seizure of goods, papers, effects, documents, etc.? We find that, as to the Federal Government, the Fourth and Fifth Amendments and, as to the States, the freedom from unconscionable invasions of privacy and the freedom from convictions based upon coerced confessions do enjoy an "intimate relation" in their perpetuation of "principles of humanity and civil liberty [secured] . . . only after years of struggle," *Bram v. United States* (1897). They express "supplementing phases of the same constitutional purpose to maintain inviolate large areas of personal privacy." *Feldman v. United States* (1944). The philosophy of each Amendment and of each freedom is complementary to, although not dependent upon, that of the other in its sphere of influence—the very least that together they assure in either sphere is that no man is to be convicted on unconstitutional evidence.

## The Exclusionary Rule

Moreover, our holding that the exclusionary rule is an essential part of both the Fourth and Fourteenth Amendments is not only the logical dictate of prior cases, but it also makes very good sense. There is no war between the Constitution and common sense. Presently, a federal prosecutor may make no use of evidence illegally seized, but a State's attorney across the street may, although he supposedly is operating under the enforceable prohibitions of the same Amendment. Thus, the

State, by admitting evidence unlawfully seized, serves to encourage disobedience to the Federal Constitution which it is bound to uphold. Moreover, as was said in *Elkins*, "[t]he very essence of a healthy federalism depends upon the avoidance of needless conflict between state and federal courts." . . .

Federal-state cooperation in the solution of crime under constitutional standards will be promoted, if only by recognition of their now mutual obligation to respect the same fundamental criteria in their approaches. . . .

Nor can it lightly be assumed that, as a practical matter, adoption of the exclusionary rule fetters law enforcement. Only last year, this Court expressly considered that contention and found that "pragmatic evidence of a sort" to the contrary was not wanting. The Court noted that "The federal courts themselves have operated under the exclusionary rule of *Weeks* for almost half a century; yet it has not been suggested either that the Federal Bureau of Investigation has thereby been rendered ineffective, or that the administration of criminal justice in the federal courts has thereby been disrupted. Moreover, the experience of the states is impressive. . . . The movement towards the rule of exclusion has been halting, but seemingly inexorable."

The ignoble shortcut to conviction left open to the State tends to destroy the entire system of constitutional restraints on which the liberties of the people rest. Having once recognized that the right to privacy embodied in the Fourth Amendment is enforceable against the States, and that the right to be secure against rude invasions of privacy by state officers is, therefore, constitutional in origin, we can no longer permit that right to remain an empty promise. Because it is enforceable in the same manner and to like effect as other basic rights secured by the Due Process Clause, we can no longer permit it to be revocable at the whim of any police officer who, in the name of law enforcement itself, chooses to suspend its enjoyment. Our decision, founded on reason and truth, gives to the individual no more than that which the Constitution guarantees him, to the police officer no less than that to which honest law enforcement is entitled, and, to the courts, that judicial integrity so necessary in the true administration of justice.

The judgment of the Supreme Court of Ohio is reversed, and the cause remanded for further proceedings not inconsistent with this opinion.

*Reversed and remanded.*

# The Due Process Clause Guarantees the Right to a Fair Trial

*Colin Evans*

*In June 1961 Earl Gideon was charged with burglary. The following selection describes his arrest and trial. During the trial Gideon was forced to serve as his own attorney because at the time, only a defendant facing capital charges was allowed a court-appointed defense attorney. While serving time for the burglary charge, Gideon wrote a letter to the Supreme Court. He asked the Court to hear his case, arguing that being denied an attorney violated his right to due process under the Fourteenth Amendment. In a rare move, the Supreme Court accepted the case. An attorney was appointed to represent Gideon, and at the conclusion of the procedures, Gideon was allowed to have his original case retried with a court-appointed attorney. Colin Evans is a writer who focuses on the judiciary and court cases.*

At eight o'clock on the morning of June 3, 1961, a patrolling police officer in Panama City, Florida, noticed that the door of the Bay Harbor Poolroom was open. Stepping inside, he saw that a cigarette machine and jukebox had been burglarized. Eyewitness testimony led to the arrest of Clarence Gideon, a 51-year-old drifter who occasionally helped out at the poolroom. He vehemently protested his innocence but two months later was placed on trial at the Panama City Courthouse. No one present had any inkling that they were about to witness history in the making.

# No Defense Lawyer

As the law then stood, Gideon, although indigent, was not automatically entitled to the services of a court-appointed defense lawyer. A 1942 Supreme Court decision, *Betts v. Brady*, extended this right only to those defendants facing a capital charge. Many states did, in fact, exceed the legal requirements and provide all felony defendants with counsel, but not Florida. Judge Robert L. McCrary, Jr. did his best to protect Gideon's interests when the trial opened August 4, 1961, but he clearly could not assume the role of advocate; that task was left to Gideon himself. Under the circumstances Gideon, a man of limited education but immense resourcefulness, performed as well as could be expected, but he was hardly the courtroom equal of Assistant State Attorney William E. Harris, who scored heavily with the testimony of Henry Cook.

This young man claimed to have seen Gideon inside the poolroom at 5:30 on the morning of the robbery. After watching Gideon for a few minutes through the window, Cook said, the defendant came out clutching a pint of wine in his hand, then made a telephone call from a nearby booth. Soon afterward a cab arrived and Gideon left.

In cross-examination Gideon sought to impugn Cook's reasons for being outside the bar at that time of the morning. Cook replied that he had "just come from a dance, down in Apalachicola—stayed out all night." A more experienced cross-examiner might have explored this potentially fruitful line of questioning, but Gideon let it pass and lapsed into a vague and argumentative discourse.

Eight witnesses testified on the defendant's behalf. None proved helpful and Clarence Gideon was found guilty. The whole trial had lasted less than one day. Three weeks later Judge McCrary sentenced Gideon to the maximum: five years imprisonment.

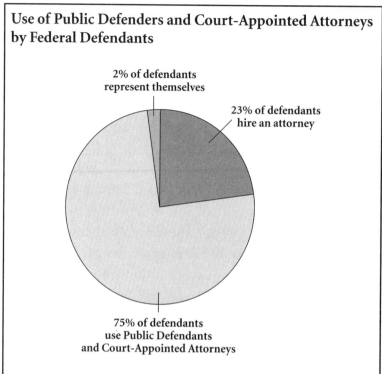

## Use of Public Defenders and Court-Appointed Attorneys by Federal Defendants

2% of defendants represent themselves

23% of defendants hire an attorney

75% of defendants use Public Defendants and Court-Appointed Attorneys

TAKEN FROM: Adam Liptak, "Gap Seen Between Court-Appointed Lawyers and Public Defenders," *New York Times*, July 13, 2007, www .nytimes.com.

## Gideon Appeals

Gideon was outraged by the verdict, particularly the fact that he had been denied counsel. He applied to the Florida Supreme Court for a writ of *habeas corpus*, an order freeing him on the ground that he was illegally imprisoned. When this application was denied Gideon penciled a five-page document entitled "Petition for a Writ of *Certiorari* Directed to the Supreme Court." (A writ of *certiorari* is an order by an appellate court to hear a particular appeal.) In other words, Gideon was asking the U.S. Supreme Court to hear his case. The suit was placed on the docket under the title *Gideon v. H.G. Cochran, Jr.*, who happened to be the director of Florida's Division of Corrections.

Each year the Supreme Court receives thousands of petitions. Most are meritless and don't get heard. Sheer weight of numbers militates [works] against the deserving remainder, and yet, against all odds, the Supreme Court decided to hear Gideon's petition. Abe Fortas, who would himself later sit on the bench, was appointed to plead Gideon's case. Responding for Cochran were Bruce R. Jacob and George Mentz. The date for oral argument was set for January 14, 1963, but before that date Mr. Cochran resigned his position with the Florida Division of Corrections. He was replaced by Louie L. Wainwright—earning for that man an enduring and wholly unwanted place in judicial history—and the case was renamed *Gideon v. Wainwright*.

## No Lawyer Equals Unfair Treatment

Fortas, arguing that the restrictive nature of *Betts v. Brady* had treated Gideon unfairly, drew a poignant analogy: "I was reminded the other night, as I was pondering this case, of Clarence Darrow when he was prosecuted for trying to fix a jury. The first thing he realized was that he needed a lawyer—he, one of the country's greatest criminal lawyers." It was time, said Fortas, for the law to change.

Needless to say, Jacob and Mentz stridently disagreed, but the mood of the times was against them, and, on March 18, 1963, the Supreme Court unanimously overruled *Betts v. Brady*, saying that all felony defendants were entitled to legal representation, irrespective of the crime charged. Justice Hugo L. Black wrote the opinion that set aside Gideon's conviction:

> [R]eason and reflection requires us to recognize that in our adversary system of criminal justice, any person haled into court, who is too poor to hire a lawyer, cannot be assured a fair trial unless counsel is provide for him. This seems to us to be an obvious truth.

## An Acquittal

On August 5, 1963, Clarence Gideon again appeared before Judge Robert L. McCrary in the Panama City Courthouse, and this time he had an experienced trial lawyer, W. Fred Turner, to defend him. All of the publicity resulted in a heavily bolstered prosecution team. In addition to William Harris, State Attorney J. Frank Adams and J. Paul Griffith were on hand to uphold the validity of the first conviction. Henry Cook was again the main prosecution witness but fared badly under Turner's incisive questioning. Particularly damaging was his admission that he had withheld details of his criminal record at the previous trial. Due in large part to Cook's poor showing, the jury acquitted Gideon of all charges.

He died in 1972 at age 61.

## Just a Letter

Because one man sat down and wrote a letter, no felony defendant need ever fear facing a court alone. *Gideon v. Wainwright* extended the law's protection to all. More than that, it gave justice a better name.

# Teenage Truancy Leads to Due Process for Students

*Abe Fortas*

*In 1966 the Supreme Court heard a case regarding due process rights for children. The following selection is the Court's opinion regarding Gerald Gault and his detention without any notice or notification to his parents. Justice Abe Fortas delivered the opinion. In the opinion Justice Fortas describes the background of the juvenile courts and the definition of a juvenile delinquent. Also discussed is a juvenile's privilege against self-incrimination and his or her right of appeal in court proceedings. Fortas served as an associate justice on the Supreme Court from 1965 to 1969.*

Mr. Justice Fortas delivered the opinion of the Court.

On Monday, June 8, 1965, at about 10 a.m., Gerald Francis Gault and a friend, Ronald Lewis, were taken into custody by the Sheriff of Gila County. Gerald was then still subject to a six months' probation order which had been entered on February 25, 1964, as a result of his having been in the company of another boy who had stolen a wallet from a lady's purse. The police action on June 8 was taken as the result of a verbal complaint by a neighbor of the boys, Mrs. Cook, about a telephone call made to her in which the caller or callers made lewd or indecent remarks. It will suffice for purposes of this opinion to say that the remarks or questions put to her were of the irritatingly, offensive, adolescent, sex variety.

At the time Gerald was picked up, his mother and father were both at work. No notice that Gerald was being taken into custody was left at the home. No other steps were taken to advise them that their son had, in effect, been arrested.

"In re Gault," U.S. Supreme Court, 387 U.S. 1, 1967. http://web.utk.edu.

Gerald was taken to the Children's Detention Home. When his mother arrived home at about 6 o'clock, Gerald was not there. Gerald's older brother was sent to look for him at the trailer home of the Lewis family. He apparently learned then that Gerald was in custody: He so informed his mother. The two of them went to the Detention Home. The deputy probation officer, Flagg, who was also superintendent of the Detention Home, told Mrs. Gault "why Jerry was there" and said that a hearing would be held in Juvenile Court at 3 o'clock the following day, June 9.

Officer Flagg filed a petition with the court on the hearing day, June 9, 1964. It was not served on the Gaults. Indeed, none of them saw this petition until the habeas corpus hearing on August 17, 1964. The petition was entirely formal. It made no reference to any factual basis for the judicial action which it initiated. It recited only that "said minor is under the age of eighteen years and is in need of the protection of this Honorable court; [and that] said minor is a delinquent minor;" it prayed for a hearing and an order regarding "the care and custody of said minor." Officer Flagg executed a formal affidavit in support of the petition.

## Conflicting Recollections

On June 9, Gerald, his mother, his older brother, and Probation Officers Flagg and Henderson appeared before the Juvenile Judge in chambers. Gerald's father was not there. He was at work out of the city. Mrs. Cook, the complainant, was not there. No one was sworn at this hearing. No transcript or recording was made. No memorandum or record of the substance of the proceedings was prepared. Our information about the proceedings and the subsequent hearing on June 15, derives entirely from the testimony of the Juvenile Court Judge, Mr. and Mrs. Gault and Officer Flagg at the habeas corpus proceeding conducted two months later. From this, it appears that at the June 9 hearing Gerald was questioned by the

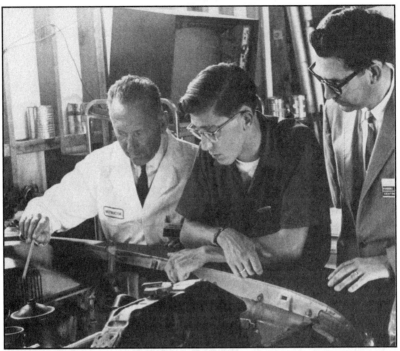

*Gerald Gault (center) at age 18, at the Parks Job Corps near Pleasanton, California, in 1967. Gault's Supreme Court case raised questions about due process rights for juveniles and resulted in a new Juvenile Courts ruling.* AP Images.

judge about the telephone call. There was conflict as to what he said. His mother recalled that Gerald said he only dialed Mrs. Cook's number and handed the telephone to his friend, Ronald. Officer Flagg recalled that Gerald had admitted making the lewd remarks. Judge McGhee testified that Gerald "admitted making one of these [lewd] statements." At the conclusion of the hearing, the judge said he would "think about it." Gerald was taken back to the Detention Home. He was not sent to his own home with his parents. On June 11 or 12, after having been detained since June 8, Gerald was released and driven home. There is no explanation in the record as to why he was kept in the Detention Home or why he was released. At 5 p.m. on the day of Gerald's release, Mrs. Gault received a note signed by Officer Flagg. It was on plain paper, not letterhead. Its entire text was as follows:

Mrs. Gault:

Judge McGhee has set Monday, June 15, 1964 at 11:00 a.m. as the date and time for further Hearings on Gerald's delinquency.

/s/Flagg

At the appointed time on Monday, June 15, Gerald, his father and mother, Ronald Lewis and his father, and Officer Flagg and Henderson were present before Judge McGhee. Witnesses at the habeas corpus proceeding differed in their recollections of Gerald's testimony at the June 15 hearing. Mr. and Mrs. Gault recalled that Gerald again testified that he had only dialed the number and that the other boy had made the remarks. Officer Flagg agreed that at this hearing Gerald did not admit making the lewd remarks. But Judge McGhee recalled that "there was some admission again of some of the lewd statements. He—he didn't admit any of the more serious lewd statements." Again, the complainant, Mrs. Cook, was not present. Mrs. Gault asked that Mrs. Cook be present "so she could see which boy that done the talking, the dirty talking over the phone." The Juvenile Judge said "she didn't have to be present at that hearing." The judge did not speak to Mrs. Cook or communicate with her at any time. Probation Officer Flagg had talked to her once—over the telephone on June 9.

## Officially a Juvenile Delinquent

At this June 15 hearing a "referral report" made by the probation officers was filed with the court, although not disclosed to Gerald or his parents. This listed the charge as "Lewd Phone Calls." At the conclusion of the hearing, the judge committed Gerald as a juvenile delinquent to the State Industrial School "for the period of his minority [that is, until 21] unless sooner discharged by due process of law." . . .

No appeal is permitted by Arizona law in juvenile cases. On August 3, 1964, a petition for a writ of habeas corpus was filed with the Supreme Court of Arizona and referred by it to the Superior Court for hearing.

At the habeas corpus hearing on August 17, Judge McGhee was vigorously cross-examined as to the basis for his actions. He testified that he had taken into account the fact that Gerald was on probation. He was asked "under what section of . . . the code you found the boy delinquent."

His answer is set forth in the margin. In substance, he concluded that Gerald came within ARS 8-201-6(a), which specifies that a "delinquent child" includes one "who has violated a law of the state or an ordinance or regulation of a political subdivision thereof." The law which Gerald was found to have violated . . . provides that a person who "in the presence of hearing of any woman or child . . . uses vulgar, abusive or obscene language, is guilty of a misdemeanor . . ." The penalty specified in the Criminal Code, which would apply to an adult, is $5 to $50, or imprisonment for not more than two months. The judge also testified that he acted under ARS 8-201-6(d) which includes in the definition of a "delinquent child" one who, as the judge phrased it, is "habitually involved in immoral matters."

Asked about this basis for his conclusion that Gerald was "habitually involved in immoral matters," the judge testified, somewhat vaguely, that two years earlier, on July 2, 1962, a "referral" was made concerning Gerald, "where the boy had stolen a baseball glove from another boy and lied to the Police Department about it." The judge said there was "no hearing," and "no accusation" relating to this incident, "because of lack of material foundation." But it seems to have remained in his mind as a relevant factor. The judge also testified that Gerald had admitted making other nuisance phone calls in the past which, as the judge recalled the boy's testimony, were "silly calls, or funny calls, or something like that."

The Superior Court dismissed the writ, and appellants sought review in the Arizona Supreme Court. . . .

## Juvenile Code of Arizona on Trial

The Supreme Court handed down an elaborate and wide-ranging opinion affirming dismissal of the writ and stated the court's conclusions as to the issues raised by appellants and other aspects of the juvenile process. In their jurisdictional statement and brief in this Court, appellants do not urge upon us all of the points passed upon by the Supreme Court of Arizona. They urge that we hold the Juvenile Code of Arizona invalid on its face or as applied in this case because, contrary to the Due Process Clause of the Fourteenth Amendment, the juvenile is taken from the custody of his parents and committed to a state institution pursuant to proceedings in which the Juvenile Court has virtually unlimited discretion, and in which the following basic rights are denied:

1. Notice of the charges;

2. Right to counsel;

3. Right to confrontation and cross-examination;

4. Privilege against self-incrimination;

5. Right to a transcript of the proceedings; and

6. Right to appellate review. . . .

From the inception of the juvenile court system, wide differences have been tolerated—indeed even insisted upon—between the procedural rights accorded to adults and those of juveniles. In practically all jurisdictions, there are rights granted to adults which are withheld from juveniles. In addition to the specific problems involved in the present case, for example, it has been held that the juvenile is not entitled to bail, to indictment by grand jury, to a public trial or to trial by jury. It is frequent practice that rules governing the arrest and interrogation of adults by the police are not observed in the case of juveniles.

## Background on Juvenile Court Movement

The history and theory underlying this development are well-known, but a recapitulation is necessary for purposes of this opinion. The juvenile court movement began in this country at the end of the last century. From the Juvenile Court statute adopted in Illinois in 1899, the system has spread to every State in the Union, the District of Columbia, and Puerto Rico. The constitutionality of Juvenile Court laws has been sustained in over 40 jurisdictions against a variety of attacks.

The early reformers were appalled by adult procedures and penalties and by the fact that children could be given long prison sentences and mixed in jails with hardened criminals. They were profoundly convinced that society's duty to the child could not be confined by the concept of justice alone. They believed that society's role was not to ascertain whether the child was "guilty" or "innocent," but "What is he, how has he become what he is, and what had best be done in his interest and in the interest of the state to save him from a downward career." The child—especially good, as they saw it—was to be made "to feel that he is the object of [the state's] care and solicitude," not that he was under arrest or on trial. The rules of criminal procedure were therefore altogether inapplicable. The apparent rigidities, technicalities, and harshness which they observed in both substantive and procedural criminal law were therefore to be discarded. The idea of crime and punishment was to be abandoned. The child was to be "treated" and "rehabilitated" and the procedures, from apprehension through institutionalization, were to be "clinical" rather than punitive.

These results were to be achieved, without coming to conceptual and constitutional grief, by insisting that the proceedings were not adversary, but that the state was proceeding as *parens patriae* [the state as parent]. The Latin phrase proved to be a great help to those who sought to rationalize the exclusion of juveniles from the constitutional scheme; but its meaning is murky and its historic credentials are of dubious relevance. The phrase was taken from chancery practice, where, however, it was used to describe the power of the state to act in loco parentis [in the place of a parent] for the purpose of protecting the property interests and the person of the child. But there is no trace of the doctrine in the history of criminal jurisprudence. At common law, children under seven were considered incapable of possessing criminal intent. Beyond that age, they were subjected to arrest, trial, and in theory to punishment like adult offenders. In these old days, the state was not deemed to have authority to accord them fewer procedural rights than adults.

The right of the state, as parens patriae, to deny to the child procedural rights available to his elders was elaborated by the assertion that a child, unlike an adult, has a right "not to liberty but to custody." He can be made to attorn to his parents, to go to school, etc. If his parents default in effective[ly] performing their custodial functions—that is, if the child is "delinquent"—the state may intervene. In doing so, it does not deprive the child of any rights, because he has none. It merely provides the "custody" to which the child is entitled. On this basis, proceedings involving juveniles were described as "civil" not "criminal" and therefore not subject to the requirements which restrict the state when it seeks to deprive a person of his liberty. . . .

Further, it is urged that the juvenile benefits from informal proceedings in the court. The early conception of the Juvenile Court proceeding was one in which a fatherly judge touched the heart and conscience of the erring youth by talking over his problems, by paternal advice and admonition, and in which, in extreme situations, benevolent and wise institutions of the State provided guidance and help "to save him from a downward career." Then, as now, goodwill and compassion were admirably prevalent. But recent studies have, with surprising unanimity, entered sharp dissent as to the validity of this gentle conception. They suggest that the appearance as well as the actuality of fairness, impartiality and orderliness—in short, the essentials of due process—may be a more impressive and more therapeutic attitude so far as the juvenile is concerned. . . .

## The Reality of the *Gault* Case

Ultimately, however, we confront the reality of that portion of the Juvenile Court process with which we deal in this case. A boy is charged with misconduct. The boy is committed to an institution where he may be restrained of liberty for years. It is of no constitutional consequence—and of limited practical meaning—that the institution to which he is committed is called an Industrial School. The fact of the matter is that, however euphemestic the title, a "receiving home" or an "industrial school" for juveniles is an institution of confinement in which the child is incarcerated for a greater or lesser time. His world becomes "a building with whitewashed walls, regimented routine and institutional hours. . . ." Instead of mother and father and sisters and brothers and friends and classmates, his world is peopled by guards, custodians, state employees, and "delinquents" confined with him for anything from waywardness to rape and homicide.

In view of this, it would be extraordinary if our Constitution did not require the procedural regularity and the exercise of care implied in the phrase "due process." Under our Constitution, the condition of being a boy does not justify a kangaroo court. The traditional ideas of Juvenile Court procedure, indeed, contemplated that time would be available and care would be used to establish precisely what the juvenile did and why he did it—was it a prank of adolescence or a brutal act threatening serious consequences to himself or society unless corrected? Under traditional notions, one would assume that in a case like that of Gerald Gault, where the juvenile appears to have a home, a working mother and father, and an older

brother, the Juvenile Judge would have made a careful inquiry
and judgment as to the possibility that the boy could be disci-
plined and dealt with at home, despite his previous transgres-
sions. Indeed, so far as appears in the record before us . . . the
points to which the judge directed his attention were little different from those that would be involved in determining any
charge of violation of a penal statute. The essential difference
between Gerald's case and a normal criminal case is that safeguards available to adults were discarded in Gerald's case. The
summary procedure as well as the long commitment was possible because Gerald was 15 years of age instead of over 18. . . .

Appellants allege that the Arizona Juvenile Code is unconstitutional or alternatively that the proceedings before the Juvenile Court were constitutionally defective because of failure
to provide adequate notice of the hearings. . . .

Notice, to comply with due process requirements, must be
given sufficiently in advance of scheduled court proceedings
so that reasonable opportunity to prepare will be afforded,
and it must "set forth the alleged misconduct with particular-
ity." It is obvious that no purpose of shielding the child from
the public stigma of knowledge of his having been taken into
custody and scheduled for hearing is served by the procedure
approved by the court below. The "initial hearing" in the
present case was a hearing on the merits. Notice at that time
is not timely; and even if there were a conceivable purpose
served by the deferral proposed by the court below, it would
have to yield to the requirements that the child and his parents or guardian be notified, in writing, of the specific charge
or factual allegations to be considered at the hearing, and that
such written notice be given at the earliest practicable time,
and in any event sufficiently in advance of the hearing to permit preparation. . . .

Appellants charge that the Juvenile Court proceedings
were fatally defective because the court did not advise Gerald
or his parents of their right to counsel, and proceeded with

the hearing, the adjudication of delinquency and the order of commitment in the absence of counsel for the child and his parents or an express waiver of the right thereto. . . . A proceeding where the issue is whether the child will be found to be "delinquent" and subjected to the loss of his liberty for years is comparable in seriousness to a felony prosecution. The juvenile needs the assistance of counsel to cope with problems of law, to make skilled inquiry into the facts, to insist upon regularity of the proceedings, and to ascertain whether he has a defense and to prepare and submit it. The child "requires the guiding hand of counsel at every step in the proceedings against him." . . .

## The Right to Due Process Extends to Juveniles

We conclude that the Due Process Clause of the Fourteenth Amendment requires that in respect of proceedings to determine delinquency which may result in commitment to an institution in which the juvenile's freedom is curtailed, the child and his parents must be notified of the child's right to be represented by counsel retained by them, or if they are unable to afford counsel, that counsel will be appointed to represent the child. . . .

Appellants urge that the writ of habeas corpus should have been granted because of the denial of the rights of confrontation and cross-examination in the Juvenile Court hearings, and because the privilege against self-incrimination was not observed. . . .

Absent a valid confession adequate to support the determination of the Juvenile Court, confrontation and sworn testimony by witnesses available for cross-examination were not essential for a finding of "delinquency." . . .

We now hold that, absent a valid confession, a determination of delinquency and an order of commitment to a state institution cannot be sustained in the absence of sworn testimony subjected to the opportunity for cross-examination in accordance with our law and constitutional requirements.

Appellants urge that the Arizona statute is unconstitutional under the Due Process Clause because, as construed by its Supreme Court, "there is no right of appeal from a juvenile court order...." The court held that there is no right to a transcript because there is no right to appeal and because the proceedings are confidential and any record must be destroyed after a prescribed period of time. Whether a transcript or other recording is made, it held, is a matter for the discretion of the juvenile court....

As the present case illustrates, the consequences of failure to provide an appeal, to record the proceedings, or to make findings or state the grounds for the juvenile court's conclusion may be to throw a burden upon the machinery for habeas corpus, to saddle the reviewing process with the burden of attempting to reconstruct a record, and to impose upon the Juvenile Judge the unseemly duty of testifying under cross-examination as to the events that transpired in the hearings before him.

For the reasons stated, the judgment of the Supreme Court of Arizona is reversed and the cause remanded for further proceedings not inconsistent with this opinion.

It is so ordered.

# Double Jeopardy and the Due Process Clause

*Elder Witt*

*In 1969 the Supreme Court ruled that because of the Fourteenth Amendment's due process clause, the double jeopardy clause of the Fifth Amendment applies not only to individuals being tried by the federal government but also to individuals being tried by the states. The following article dissects the double jeopardy clause and explains how it pertains to situations involving the federal government, a state government, or both. In 1937 the Supreme Court decided that the Fourteenth Amendment due process clause did not apply to state government double jeopardy actions. However, in 1969 the Court overruled this decision.* Congressional Quarterly *is a political journal covering Congress and other aspects of politics.*

To restrain the government from repeated prosecutions of an individual for one particular offense, the prohibition against double jeopardy was included in the Fifth Amendment. The Supreme Court has held that this guarantee protects an individual both against multiple prosecutions for the same offense and against multiple punishments for the same crime.

Until 1969 the double jeopardy clause applied only to federal prosecutions. In that year the Supreme Court in *Benton v. Maryland* held that the due process guarantee of the Fourteenth Amendment extended this protection to persons tried by states as well.

## Double Jeopardy Defined

A defendant is placed in jeopardy at the time his jury is sworn in, although if a mistrial is declared under certain circum-

Elder Witt, *Congressional Quarterly's Guide to the U.S. Supreme Court*, Washington, DC: Congressional Quarterly, 1990. Copyright © 1990 by CQ Press, published by CQ Press, a division of SAGE Publications. Reproduced by permission.

stances or if the jury fails to agree on a verdict, the double jeopardy clause does not forbid his retrial.

If he is convicted, he may waive his immunity against double jeopardy and seek a new trial, or he may appeal the verdict to a higher court. If the conviction is set aside for a reason other than insufficient evidence, he may be tried again for the same offense.

If he is acquitted, the double jeopardy clause absolutely bars any further prosecution of him for that crime, even if the acquittal was the result of error.

## Federal and State Prosecutions

The double jeopardy guarantee, however, protects only against repeated prosecutions by a single sovereign government. Thus, it is not violated when a person is tried on both state and federal charges arising from a single offense. Many acts are offenses under both federal and state laws.

The Court established this rule in the 1922 case of *United States v. Lanza*. Lanza was convicted for violating Washington State's prohibition law. Then he was indicted on the same grounds for violating the federal prohibition law. The federal district judge dismissed his indictment as a violation of the double jeopardy guarantee. The government appealed the dismissal, and the Supreme Court reversed it, 6–3.

Chief Justice William Howard Taft wrote:

We have here two sovereignties, deriving power from different sources, capable of dealing with the same subject-matter within the same territory. Each may, without interference by the other, enact laws to secure prohibition. . . . Each government, in determining what shall be an offense against its peace and dignity, is exercising its own sovereignty, not that of the other.

It follows that an act denounced as a crime by both national and state sovereignties is an offense against the peace and dignity of both, and may be punished by each. The 5th Amendment, like all the other guaranties in the first eight amendments, applies only to proceedings by the Federal government ... and the double jeopardy therein forbidden is a second prosecution under authority of the Federal government after a first trial for the same offense under the same authority. Here the same act was an offense against the state of Washington, because a violation of its law, and also an offense against the United States under the National Prohibition Act. The defendants thus committed two different offenses by the same act, and a conviction by a court of Washington of the offense against that state is not a conviction of the different offense against the United States, and so is not double jeopardy.

The *Lanza* rule survives. In 1959 and again in 1985 the Court reaffirmed its opinion that multiple prosecutions by different sovereigns—including two states—for the same offense did not violate the double jeopardy clause. However, because a state and a city are not separate sovereigns, the double jeopardy guarantee does protect an individual against prosecution by both for one offense.

The separate sovereignties doctrine was applied by the Court in the 1978 case of *United States v. Wheeler*. There the Court ruled that the double jeopardy clause did not protect an American Indian defendant convicted in tribal court from being tried by federal authorities for the same offense.

In 1985 the Court ruled against a defendant's challenge to being tried in two different states for two parts of the same crime—the murder of his wife. One state—where the murder was committed—charged him for the murder; the second— where he dumped the body—charged him for that crime. The Supreme Court, with Justice Sandra Day O'Connor writing the opinion in *Heath v. Alabama*, found nothing to violate the double jeopardy guarantee.

## The Risk of Lesser Charges

The double jeopardy clause also protects an individual who successfully appeals his conviction on a lesser charge from being retried on the original charge.

In the 1957 case of *Green v. United States* the Court ruled that Green, tried for first-degree murder but convicted of murder in the second degree—a verdict that he successfully appealed—could not be tried again for first-degree murder after he won a new trial on appeal. The Court said that Green had been once in jeopardy for first-degree murder and that appeal of his conviction for a different crime did not constitute a waiver of his protection against double jeopardy. The Court explained:

> The underlying idea, one that is deeply ingrained in at least the Anglo-American system of jurisprudence, is that the State with all its resources and power should not be allowed to make repeated attempts to convict an individual for an alleged offense, thereby subjecting him to embarrassment, expense and ordeal and compelling him to live in a continuing state of anxiety and insecurity, as well as enhancing the possibility that even though innocent he may be found guilty.

## Due Process Does Not Apply

In 1937—in the often-cited decision in *Palko v. Connecticut*—the Court rejected the idea that the Fourteenth Amendment due process clause applied the double jeopardy guarantee to state action.

Palko was convicted of second-degree murder and sentenced to life imprisonment. The state sought and won a new trial claiming that legal errors had occurred at trial. At a second trial Palko was found guilty of first-degree murder and sentenced to die. He challenged his second conviction as a violation of the double jeopardy guarantee and of due process.

The Court rejected this argument, excluding the double jeopardy guarantee from the list of guarantees that had been "absorbed" into due process. That protection, Justice Benjamin N. Cardozo wrote for the majority, was not "of the very essence of a scheme of ordered liberty." He then elaborated:

> Is that kind of double jeopardy to which the statute has subjected him a hardship so acute and shocking that our polity will not endure it? Does it violate those "fundamental principles of liberty and justice which lie at the base of all our civil and political institutions?" . . . The answer surely must be "no." . . . The state is not attempting to wear the accused out by a multitude of cases with accumulated trials. It asks no more than this, that the case against him shall go on until there shall be a trial free from the corrosion of substantial legal error. . . . This is not cruelty at all, nor even vexation in any immoderate degree. If the trial had been infected with error adverse to the accused, there might have been review at his instance, and as often as necessary to purge the vicious taint. A reciprocal privilege, subject at all times to the discretion of the presiding judge . . . has now been granted to the state. There is here no seismic innovation. The edifice of justice stands, its symmetry, to many, greater than before.

## Due Process Does Apply

Thirty-two years later, in 1969, the Court overruled *Palko*. In its last announced decision under Chief Justice Earl Warren, the Court in *Benton v. Maryland* declared that the double jeopardy clause did apply to the states through the due process guarantee of the Fourteenth Amendment. Justice Thurgood Marshall delivered the majority opinion:

> Our recent cases have thoroughly rejected the *Palko* notion that basic constitutional rights can be denied by the States so long as the totality of the circumstances does not disclose a denial of "fundamental fairness." Once it is decided that a

particular Bill of Rights guarantee is "fundamental to the American scheme of justice," ... the same constitutional standards apply against both the State and Federal Governments. *Palko's* roots had thus been cut away years ago. We today only recognize the inevitable.

Justices John Marshall Harlan and Potter Stewart dissented from this "march toward 'incorporating' much, if not all, of the Federal Bill of Rights into the Due Process Clause."

A dozen years later, a case similar to *Palko* came to the Court. *Bullington v. Missouri* arose after Robert Bullington was convicted of murder, for which he could have been sentenced to death. Instead, the jury sentenced him to life in prison without eligibility for parole for fifty years.

Bullington won a new trial, and the state declared that it would again seek a death sentence for him. Bullington objected, arguing that the double jeopardy clause precluded his being once again placed in jeopardy of a death sentence—after a jury had already decided that he should not be executed.

The Supreme Court, 5–4, agreed with him. The state should not have a second chance to try to convince a jury to sentence Bullington to die, wrote Justice Harry A. Blackmun. Once a jury had decided that he should not die for his crime, Bullington's right to be secure against double jeopardy forbade the state, even at a new trial, to seek the death penalty. Dissenting were Chief Justice Warren E. Burger and Justices Byron R. White, Lewis P. Powell, Jr., and William H. Rehnquist.

# Due Process Protects a Woman's Right to Choose Abortion

*Harry Blackmun*

*Most individuals see the landmark abortion case* Roe v. Wade *as a question of morality. When handing down the Court's opinion, Justice Harry Blackmun wrote that the Court would not "resolve the difficult question of when life begins. When those trained in the respective disciplines of medicine, philosophy, and theology are unable to arrive at any consensus, the judiciary, at this point in the development of man's knowledge, is not in a position to speculate as to this answer." The Supreme Court saw abortion as an issue of personal privacy, which is protected by the due process clause of the Fourteenth Amendment. In the following selection, this right of privacy for a woman contemplating abortion is spelled out depending on how far along she is in her pregnancy. The question of the definition of "person," according to the Constitution and in reference to the Fourteenth Amendment, is also discussed. Blackmun served on the Supreme Court from 1970 to 1994.*

Mr. Justice Blackmun delivered the opinion of the Court.

This Texas federal appeal and its Georgia companion, *Doe v. Bolton*, present constitutional challenges to state criminal abortion legislation. The Texas statutes under attack here are typical of those that have been in effect in many States for approximately a century. The Georgia statutes, in contrast, have a modern cast, and are a legislative product that, to an extent at least, obviously reflects the influences of recent attitudinal

Harry Blackmun, "Transcript of a Supreme Court Decision: Due Process Protects a Woman's Right to Choose Abortion," in Legal Information Institute, Cornell University Law School, January 22, 1973. www.law.cornell.edu/supct/index.html.

change, of advancing medical knowledge and techniques, and of new thinking about an old issue.

We forthwith acknowledge our awareness of the sensitive and emotional nature of the abortion controversy, of the vigorous opposing views, even among physicians, and of the deep and seemingly absolute convictions that the subject inspires. One's philosophy, one's experiences, one's exposure to the raw edges of human existence, one's religious training, one's attitudes toward life and family and their values, and the moral standards one establishes and seeks to observe, are all likely to influence and to color one's thinking and conclusions about abortion.

In addition, population growth, pollution, poverty, and racial overtones tend to complicate and not to simplify the problem.

Our task, of course, is to resolve the issue by constitutional measurement, free of emotion and of predilection. We seek earnestly to do this, and, because we do, we have inquired into, and in this opinion place some emphasis upon, medical and medical-legal history and what that history reveals about man's attitudes toward the abortion procedure over the centuries. We bear in mind, too, Mr. Justice [Oliver Wendell] Holmes [Jr.]'[s] admonition in his now-vindicated dissent in *Lochner v. New York* (1905):

> [The Constitution] is made for people of fundamentally differing views, and the accident of our finding certain opinions natural and familiar or novel and even shocking ought not to conclude our judgment upon the question whether statutes embodying them conflict with the Constitution of the United States.

The Texas statutes that concern us here are Arts. 1191– 1194 and 1196 of the State's Penal Code. These make it a crime to "procure an abortion," as therein defined, or to attempt one, except with respect to "an abortion procured or at-

*Attorney Sarah Weddington (left) on the day she defended Jane Roe in the case of* Roe v. Wade *with then Texas congressman George Mahon, who supported Weddington's case.* Courtesy of Sarah Weddington. Reproduced by permission.

tempted by medical advice for the purpose of saving the life of the mother." Similar statutes are in existence in a majority of the States. . . .

## Background on Jane Roe and James Hallford

Jane Roe, a single woman who was residing in Dallas County, Texas, instituted this federal action in March 1970 against the District Attorney of the county. She sought a declaratory

judgment that the Texas criminal abortion statutes were unconstitutional on their face, and an injunction restraining the
defendant from enforcing the statutes.

Roe alleged that she was unmarried and pregnant; that she
wished to terminate her pregnancy by an abortion "performed
by a competent, licensed physician, under safe, clinical conditions"; that she was unable to get a "legal" abortion in Texas
because her life did not appear to be threatened by the con-
tinuation of her pregnancy; and that she could not afford to
travel to another jurisdiction in order to secure a legal abortion under safe conditions. She claimed that the Texas statutes
were unconstitutionally vague and that they abridged her
right of personal privacy, protected by the First, Fourth, Fifth,
Ninth, and Fourteenth Amendments. By an amendment to
her complaint, Roe purported to sue "on behalf of herself and
all other women" similarly situated.

James Hubert Hallford, a licensed physician, sought and
was granted leave to intervene in Roe's action. In his complaint, he alleged that he had been arrested previously for violations of the Texas abortion statutes, and that two such prosecutions were pending against him. He described conditions
of patients who came to him seeking abortions, and he
claimed that for many cases he, as a physician, was unable to
determine whether they fell within or outside the exception
recognized by Article 1196. He alleged that, as a consequence,
the statutes were vague and uncertain, in violation of the
Fourteenth Amendment, and that they violated his own and
his patients' rights to privacy in the doctor-patient relationship and his own right to practice medicine, rights he claimed
were guaranteed by the First, Fourth, Fifth, Ninth, and Fourteenth Amendments. . . .

On the merits, the District Court held that the

> fundamental right of single women and married persons to
> choose whether to have children is protected by the Ninth
> Amendment, through the Fourteenth Amendment,

and that the Texas criminal abortion statutes were void on their face because they were both unconstitutionally vague and constituted an overbroad infringement of the plaintiffs' Ninth Amendment rights. . . .

The principal thrust of appellant's attack on the Texas statutes is that they improperly invade a right, said to be possessed by the pregnant woman, to choose to terminate her pregnancy. Appellant would discover this right in the concept of personal "liberty" embodied in the Fourteenth Amendment's Due Process Clause; or in personal, marital, familial, and sexual privacy said to be protected by the Bill of Rights or its penumbras. . . .

## History of Abortion Laws

It perhaps is not generally appreciated that the restrictive criminal abortion laws in effect in a majority of States today are of relatively recent vintage. Those laws, generally proscribing abortion or its attempt at any time during pregnancy except when necessary to preserve the pregnant woman's life, are not of ancient or even of common law origin. Instead, they derive from statutory changes effected, for the most part, in the latter half of the 19th century. . . .

In this country, the law in effect in all but a few States until mid-19th century was the preexisting English common law. Connecticut, the first State to enact abortion legislation, adopted in 1821 that part of Lord Ellenborough's Act that related to a woman "quick with child." The death penalty was not imposed. Abortion before quickening was made a crime in that State only in 1860. In 1828, New York enacted legislation that, in two respects, was to serve as a model for early anti-abortion statutes. First, while barring destruction of an unquickened fetus as well as a quick fetus, it made the former only a misdemeanor, but the latter second-degree manslaughter. Second, it incorporated a concept of therapeutic abortion by providing that an abortion was excused if it shall have been necessary to preserve the life of such mother, or shall have been advised by two physicians to be necessary for such purpose.

By 1840, when Texas had received the common law, only eight American States had statutes dealing with abortion. It was not until after the War Between the States that legislation began generally to replace the common law. Most of these initial statutes dealt severely with abortion after quickening, but were lenient with it before quickening. Most punished attempts equally with completed abortions. While many statutes included the exception for an abortion thought by one or more physicians to be necessary to save the mother's life, that provision soon disappeared, and the typical law required that the procedure actually be necessary for that purpose. Gradually, in the middle and late 19th century, the quickening distinction disappeared from the statutory law of most States and the degree of the offense and the penalties were increased. By the end of the 1950's, a large majority of the jurisdictions banned abortion, however and whenever performed, unless done to save or preserve the life of the mother. The exceptions, Alabama and the District of Columbia, permitted abortion to preserve the mother's health. Three States permitted abortions that were not "unlawfully" performed or that were not "without lawful justification," leaving interpretation of those standards to the courts. In the past several years, however, a trend toward liberalization of abortion statutes has resulted in adoption, by about one-third of the States, of less stringent laws. . . .

It is thus apparent that, at common law, at the time of the adoption of our Constitution, and throughout the major portion of the 19th century, abortion was viewed with less disfavor than under most American statutes currently in effect. Phrasing it another way, a woman enjoyed a substantially broader right to terminate a pregnancy than she does in most States today. At least with respect to the early stage of pregnancy, and very possibly without such a limitation, the opportunity to make this choice was present in this country well into the 19th century. Even later, the law continued for some time to treat less punitively an abortion procured in early pregnancy. . . .

# The Continued Existence of Abortion Laws

Three reasons have been advanced to explain historically the enactment of criminal abortion laws in the 19th century and to justify their continued existence.

It has been argued occasionally that these laws were the product of a Victorian social concern to discourage illicit sexual conduct. Texas, however, does not advance this justification in the present case, and it appears that no court or commentator has taken the argument seriously. The appellants and *amici* [friends] contend, moreover, that this is not a proper state purpose, at all and suggest that, if it were, the Texas statutes are overbroad in protecting it, since the law fails to distinguish between married and unwed mothers.

A second reason is concerned with abortion as a medical procedure. When most criminal abortion laws were first enacted, the procedure was a hazardous one for the woman. This was particularly true prior to the development of antisepsis. Antiseptic techniques, of course, were based on discoveries by [Joseph] Lister, [Louis] Pasteur, and others first announced in 1867, but were not generally accepted and employed until about the turn of the century. Abortion mortality was high. Even after 1900, and perhaps until as late as the development of antibiotics in the 1940's, standard modern techniques such as dilation and curettage were not nearly so safe as they are today. Thus, it has been argued that a State's real concern in enacting a criminal abortion law was to protect the pregnant woman, that is, to restrain her from submitting to a procedure that placed her life in serious jeopardy.

Modern medical techniques have altered this situation. Appellants and various *amici* refer to medical data indicating that abortion in early pregnancy, that is, prior to the end of the first trimester, although not without its risk, is now relatively safe. Mortality rates for women undergoing early abortions, where the procedure is legal, appear to be as low as or lower than the rates for normal childbirth. Consequently, any interest of the State in protecting the woman from an inherently hazardous procedure, except when it would be equally dangerous for her to forgo it, has largely disappeared. Of course, important state interests in the areas of health and medical standards do remain. The State has a legitimate interest in seeing to it that abortion, like any other medical procedure, is performed under circumstances that insure maximum safety for the patient. This interest obviously extends at least to the performing physician and his staff, to the facilities involved, to the availability of after-care, and to adequate provision for any complication or emergency that might arise. The prevalence of high mortality rates at illegal "abortion mills" strengthens, rather than weakens, the State's interest in regulating the conditions under which abortions are performed. Moreover, the risk to the woman increases as her pregnancy continues. Thus, the State retains a definite interest in protecting the woman's own health and safety when an abortion is proposed at a late stage of pregnancy.

The third reason is the State's interest—some phrase it in terms of duty—in protecting prenatal life. Some of the argument for this justification rests on the theory that a new human life is present from the moment of conception. The State's interest and general obligation to protect life then extends, it is argued, to prenatal life. Only when the life of the pregnant mother herself is at stake, balanced against the life she carries within her, should the interest of the embryo or fetus not prevail. Logically, of course, a legitimate state interest in this area need not stand or fall on acceptance of the belief that life begins at conception or at some other point prior to live birth. In assessing the State's interest, recognition may be given to the less rigid claim that as long as at least potential life is involved, the State may assert interests beyond the protection of the pregnant woman alone.

Parties challenging state abortion laws have sharply disputed in some courts the contention that a purpose of these laws, when enacted, was to protect prenatal life. Pointing to the absence of legislative history to support the contention, they claim that most state laws were designed solely to protect the woman. Because medical advances have lessened this concern, at least with respect to abortion in early pregnancy, they argue that with respect to such abortions the laws can no longer be justified by any state interest. There is some scholarly support for this view of original purpose. The few state courts called upon to interpret their laws in the late 19th and early 20th centuries did focus on the State's interest in protecting the woman's health, rather than in preserving the embryo and fetus. Proponents of this view point out that in many States, including Texas, by statute or judicial interpretation, the pregnant woman herself could not be prosecuted for self-abortion or for cooperating in an abortion performed upon her by another. They claim that adoption of the "quickening" distinction through received common law and state statutes tacitly recognizes the greater health hazards inherent in late abortion and impliedly repudiates the theory that life begins at conception.

It is with these interests, and the eight to be attached to them, that this case is concerned.

## The Right of Privacy

The Constitution does not explicitly mention any right of privacy. In a line of decisions, however, ... the Court has recognized that a right of personal privacy, or a guarantee of certain areas or zones of privacy, does exist under the Constitution. . . .

This right of privacy, whether it be founded in the Fourteenth Amendment's concept of personal liberty and restrictions upon state action, as we feel it is, or, as the District Court determined, in the Ninth Amendment's reservation of rights to the people, is broad enough to encompass a woman's decision whether or not to terminate her pregnancy. The detriment that the State would impose upon the pregnant woman by denying this choice altogether is apparent. Specific and direct harm medically diagnosable even in early pregnancy may be involved. Maternity, or additional offspring, may force upon the woman a distressful life and future. Psychological harm may be imminent. Mental and physical health may be taxed by child care. There is also the distress, for all concerned, associated with the unwanted child, and there is the problem of bringing a child into a family already unable, psychologically and otherwise, to care for it. In other cases, as in this one, the additional difficulties and continuing stigma of unwed motherhood may be involved. All these are factors the woman and her responsible physician necessarily will consider in consultation.

## No Broad Rights to Abortion

On the basis of elements such as these, appellant and some *amici* argue that the woman's right is absolute and that she is entitled to terminate her pregnancy at whatever time, in whatever way, and for whatever reason she alone chooses. With this we do not agree. Appellant's arguments that Texas either has no valid interest at all in regulating the abortion decision, or no interest strong enough to support any limitation upon the woman's sole determination, are unpersuasive. The Court's decisions recognizing a right of privacy also acknowledge that some state regulation in areas protected by that right is appropriate. As noted above, a State may properly assert important interests in safeguarding health, in maintaining medical standards, and in protecting potential life. At some point in pregnancy, these respective interests become sufficiently compelling to sustain regulation of the factors that govern the abortion decision. The privacy right involved, therefore, cannot be said to be absolute. In fact, it is not clear to us that the claim asserted by some *amici* that one has an unlimited right to do with one's body as one pleases bears a close relationship to the right of privacy previously articulated in the Court's decisions. The Court has refused to recognize an unlimited right of this kind in the past.

We, therefore, conclude that the right of personal privacy includes the abortion decision, but that this right is not unqualified, and must be considered against important state interests in regulation. . . .

Although the results are divided, most . . . courts have agreed that the right of privacy, however based, is broad enough to cover the abortion decision; that the right, nonetheless, is not absolute, and is subject to some limitations; and that, at some point, the state interests as to protection of health, medical standards, and prenatal life, become dominant. We agree with this approach. . . .

Courts sustaining state laws have held that the State's determinations to protect health or prenatal life are dominant and constitutionally justifiable. . . .

## Constitutional Definition of "Person"

The appellee and certain *amici* argue that the fetus is a "person" within the language and meaning of the Fourteenth Amendment. In support of this, they outline at length and in detail the well known facts of fetal development. If this suggestion of personhood is established, the appellant's case, of course, collapses, for the fetus' right to life would then be guaranteed specifically by the Amendment. The appellant conceded as much on reargument. On the other hand, the appellee conceded on reargument that no case could be cited that holds that a fetus is a person within the meaning of the Fourteenth Amendment.

The Constitution does not define "person" in so many words. Section 1 of the Fourteenth Amendment contains three references to "person." The first, in defining "citizens," speaks of "persons born or naturalized in the United States." The word also appears both in the Due Process Clause and in the Equal Protection Clause. "Person" is used in other places in the Constitution: in the listing of qualifications for Representatives and Senators, Art. I, § 2, cl. 2, and § 3, cl. 3; in the Apportionment Clause, Art. 1, § 2, cl. 3; in the Migration and Importation provision, Art. I, § 9, cl. 1; in the Emolument Clause, Art. I, § 9, cl. 8; in the Electors provisions, Art. II, § 1, cl. 2, and the superseded cl. 3; in the provision outlining qualifications for the office of President, Art. II, § 1, cl. 5; in the Extradition provisions, Art. IV, § 2, cl. 2, and the superseded Fugitive Slave Clause 3; and in the Fifth, Twelfth, and Twenty-second Amendments, as well as in §§ 2 and 3 of the Fourteenth Amendment. But in nearly all these instances, the use of the word is such that it has application only postnatally. None indicates, with any assurance, that it has any possible pre-natal application.

All this, together with our observation, *supra* [judgment or decision], that, throughout the major portion of the 19th century, prevailing legal abortion practices were far freer than they are today, persuades us that the word "person," as used in the Fourteenth Amendment, does not include the unborn. This is in accord with the results reached in those few cases where the issue has been squarely presented.... Indeed, our decision in *United States v. Vuitch* inferentially is to the same effect, for we there would not have indulged in statutory interpretation favorable to abortion in specified circumstances if the necessary consequence was the termination of life entitled to Fourteenth Amendment protection.

This conclusion, however, does not of itself fully answer the contentions raised by Texas, and we pass on to other considerations.

## Pregnancy and Privacy

The pregnant woman cannot be isolated in her privacy. She carries an embryo and, later, a fetus, if one accepts the medical definitions of the developing young in the human uterus.... As we have intimated above, it is reasonable and appropriate for a State to decide that, at some point in time another interest, that of health of the mother or that of potential human life, becomes significantly involved. The woman's privacy is no longer sole and any right of privacy she possesses must be measured accordingly.

Texas urges that, apart from the Fourteenth Amendment, life begins at conception and is present throughout pregnancy, and that, therefore, the State has a compelling interest in protecting that life from and after conception. We need not resolve the difficult question of when life begins. When those trained in the respective disciplines of medicine, philosophy, and theology are unable to arrive at any consensus, the judiciary, at this point in the development of man's knowledge, is not in a position to speculate as to the answer.

## Viability of a Fetus

It should be sufficient to note briefly the wide divergence of thinking on this most sensitive and difficult question. There has always been strong support for the view that life does not begin until live birth. This was the belief of the Stoics [followers of the Greek philosopher Zeno]. It appears to be the predominant, though not the unanimous, attitude of the Jewish faith. It may be taken to represent also the position of a large segment of the Protestant community, insofar as that can be ascertained; organized groups that have taken a formal position on the abortion issue have generally regarded abortion as a matter for the conscience of the individual and her family.

As we have noted, the common law found greater significance in quickening. Physician[s] and their scientific colleagues have regarded that event with less interest and have tended to focus either upon conception, upon live birth, or upon the interim point at which the fetus becomes "viable," that is, potentially able to live outside the mother's womb, albeit with artificial aid. Viability is usually placed at about seven months (28 weeks) but may occur earlier, even at 24 weeks. The Aristotelian theory of "mediate animation," that held sway throughout the Middle Ages and the Renaissance in Europe, continued to be official Roman Catholic dogma until the 19th century, despite opposition to this "ensoulment" theory from those in the Church who would recognize the existence of life from the moment of conception. The latter is now, of course, the official belief of the Catholic Church. As one brief *amicus* discloses, this is a view strongly held by many non-Catholics as well, and by many physicians. Substantial problems for precise definition of this view are posed, however, by new embryological data that purport to indicate that conception is a "process" over time, rather than an event, and by new medical techniques such as menstrual extraction, the "morning-after" pill, implantation of embryos, artificial insemination, and even artificial wombs.

In areas other than criminal abortion, the law has been reluctant to endorse any theory that life, as we recognize it, begins before live birth, or to accord legal rights to the unborn except in narrowly defined situations and except when the rights are contingent upon live birth. For example, the traditional rule of tort law denied recovery for prenatal injuries even though the child was born alive. That rule has been changed in almost every jurisdiction. In most States, recovery is said to be permitted only if the fetus was viable, or at least quick, when the injuries were sustained, though few courts have squarely so held. In a recent development, generally opposed by the commentators, some States permit the parents of a stillborn child to maintain an action for wrongful death because of prenatal injuries. Such an action, however, would appear to be one to vindicate the parents' interest and is thus consistent with the view that the fetus, at most, represents only the potentiality of life. Similarly, unborn children have been recognized as acquiring rights or interests by way of inheritance or other devolution of property, and have been represented by guardians *ad litem* [party in a lawsuit appointed to act on behalf of another party]. Perfection of the interests involved, again, has generally been contingent upon live birth. In short, the unborn have never been recognized in the law as persons in the whole sense.

## Legitimate Interests of the State

In view of all this, we do not agree that, by adopting one theory of life, Texas may override the rights of the pregnant woman that are at stake. We repeat, however, that the State does have an important and legitimate interest in preserving and protecting the health of the pregnant woman, whether she be a resident of the State or a nonresident who seeks medical consultation and treatment there, and that it has still another important and legitimate interest in protecting the potentiality of human life. These interests are separate and distinct. Each grows in substantiality as the woman approaches term and, at a point during pregnancy, each becomes "compelling."

With respect to the State's important and legitimate interest in the health of the mother, the "compelling" point, in the light of present medical knowledge, is at approximately the end of the first trimester. This is so because of the now-established medical fact, . . . that, until the end of the first trimester mortality in abortion may be less than mortality in normal childbirth. It follows that, from and after this point, a State may regulate the abortion procedure to the extent that the regulation reasonably relates to the preservation and protection of maternal health. Examples of permissible state regulation in this area are requirements as to the qualifications of the person who is to perform the abortion; as to the licensure of that person; as to the facility in which the procedure is to be performed, that is, whether it must be a hospital or may be a clinic or some other place of less-than-hospital status; as to the licensing of the facility; and the like.

This means, on the other hand, that, for the period of pregnancy prior to this "compelling" point, the attending physician, in consultation with his patient, is free to determine, without regulation by the State, that, in his medical judgment, the patient's pregnancy should be terminated. If that decision is reached, the judgment may be effectuated by an abortion free of interference by the State.

With respect to the State's important and legitimate interest in potential life, the "compelling" point is at viability. This is so because the fetus then presumably has the capability of meaningful life outside the mother's womb. State regulation protective of fetal life after viability thus has both logical and biological justifications. If the State is interested in protecting fetal life after viability, it may go so far as to proscribe abortion during that period, except when it is necessary to preserve the life or health of the mother.

Measured against these standards, Art. 1196 of the Texas Penal Code, in restricting legal abortions to those "procured or attempted by medical advice for the purpose of saving the life of the mother," sweeps too broadly. The statute makes no distinction between abortions performed early in pregnancy and those performed later, and it limits to a single reason, "saving" the mother's life, the legal justification for the procedure. The statute, therefore, cannot survive the constitutional attack made upon it here. . . .

## Conclusions of the Court

Our conclusion that Art. 1196 is unconstitutional means, of course, that the Texas abortion statutes, as a unit, must fall.

The exception of Art. 1196 cannot be struck down separately, for then the State would be left with a statute proscribing all abortion procedures no matter how medically urgent the case.

Although the District Court granted appellant Roe declaratory relief, it stopped short of issuing an injunction against enforcement of the Texas statutes. The Court has recognized that different considerations enter into a federal court's decision as to declaratory relief, on the one hand, and injunctive relief, on the other. . . .

*It is so ordered.*

# Due Process Should Not Protect Woman's Right to Choose Abortion

*William H. Rehnquist*

*The landmark Supreme Court case* Roe v. Wade *has been the cause of much controversy since the decision was handed down in January 1973. A woman's right to choose whether to have an abortion has been either loudly cheered or equally loudly vilified. Justice William H. Rehnquist did not agree that a woman has the right to choose and wrote the dissenting opinion. In this opinion, contained in the following selection, Rehnquist discusses the question of trimesters of pregnancy and how it relates to the restrictions that a state may place on an individual. He also talks about the intent of the Fourteenth Amendment and the limits of the due process clause in relation to the abortion question. Rehnquist was a Supreme Court justice from 1972 until his death in 2005. He became chief justice in 1986.*

Mr. Justice Rehnquist, dissenting.

The Court's opinion brings to the decision of this troubling question both extensive historical fact and a wealth of legal scholarship. While the opinion thus commands my respect, I find myself nonetheless in fundamental disagreement with those parts of it that invalidate the Texas statute in question, and therefore dissent.

## The First Trimester Question

The Court's opinion decides that a State may impose virtually no restriction on the performance of abortions during the first trimester of pregnancy. Our previous decisions indicate

William H. Rehnquist, III, "*Roe v. Wade* (Appeal from the United States District Court for the Northern District of Texas)," U.S. Supreme Court, 410 U.S. 113, 1973. http:// supreme.justia.com.

that a necessary predicate for such an opinion is a plaintiff who was in her first trimester of pregnancy at some time during the pendency of her lawsuit. While a party may vindicate his own constitutional rights, he may not seek vindication for the rights of others. The Court's statement of facts in this case makes clear, however, that the record in no way indicates the presence of such a plaintiff. We know only that plaintiff Roe at the time of filing her complaint was a pregnant woman; for aught that appears in this record, she may have been in her last trimester of pregnancy as of the date the complaint was filed.

Nothing in the Court's opinion indicates that Texas might not constitutionally apply its proscription of abortion as written to a woman in that stage of pregnancy. Nonetheless, the Court uses her complaint against the Texas statute as a fulcrum for deciding that States may impose virtually no restrictions on medical abortions performed during the first trimester of pregnancy. In deciding such a hypothetical lawsuit, the Court departs from the longstanding admonition that it should never "formulate a rule of constitutional law broader than is required by the precise facts to which it is to be applied." *Liverpool, New York & Philadelphia S.S. Co. v. Commissioners of Emigration* (1885).

## The Limits of the Due Process Clause

Even if there were a plaintiff in this case capable of litigating the issue which the Court decides, I would reach a conclusion opposite to that reached by the Court. I have difficulty in concluding, as the Court does, that the right of "privacy" is involved in this case. Texas, by the statute here challenged, bars the performance of a medical abortion by a licensed physician on a plaintiff such as Roe. A transaction resulting in an operation such as this is not "private" in the ordinary usage of that word. Nor is the "privacy" that the Court finds here even a distant relative of the freedom from searches and seizures protected by the Fourth Amendment to the Constitution, which the Court has referred to as embodying a right to privacy.

If the Court means by the term "privacy" no more than that the claim of a person to be free from unwanted state regulation of consensual [agreeing] transactions may be a form of "liberty" protected by the Fourteenth Amendment, there is no doubt that similar claims have been upheld in our earlier decisions on the basis of that liberty. I agree with the statement of MR. JUSTICE STEWART in his concurring opinion that the "liberty," against deprivation of which without due process the Fourteenth Amendment protects, embraces more than the rights found in the Bill of Rights. But that liberty is not guaranteed absolutely against deprivation, only against deprivation without due process of law. The test traditionally applied in the area of social and economic legislation is whether or not a law such as that challenged has a rational relation to a valid state objective. The Due Process Clause of the Fourteenth Amendment undoubtedly does place a limit, albeit a broad one, on legislative power to enact laws such as this. If the Texas statute were to prohibit an abortion even where the mother's life is in jeopardy, I have little doubt that such a statute would lack a rational relation to a valid state objective under the test stated in *Williamson [v. Lee]*. But the Court's sweeping invalidation of any restrictions on abortion during the first trimester is impossible to justify under that standard, and the conscious weighing of competing factors that the Court's opinion apparently substitutes for the established test is far more appropriate to a legislative judgment than to a judicial one.

The Court eschews the history of the Fourteenth Amendment in its reliance on the "compelling state interest" test. But the Court adds a new wrinkle to this test by transposing it from the legal considerations associated with the Equal Protection Clause of the Fourteenth Amendment to this case arising under the Due Process Clause of the Fourteenth Amendment. Unless I misapprehend the consequences of this transplanting of the "compelling state interest test," the Court's opinion will accomplish the seemingly impossible feat of leaving this area of the law more confused than it found it.

## The Intent of the Fourteenth Amendment

While the Court's opinion quotes from the dissent of Mr. Justice [Oliver Wendell] Holmes [Jr.] in *Lochner v. New York* (1905), the result it reaches is more closely attuned to the majority opinion of Mr. Justice [Rufus W.] Peckham in that case. As in *Lochner* and similar cases applying substantive due process standards to economic and social welfare legislation, the adoption of the compelling state interest standard will inevitably require this Court to examine the legislative policies and pass on the wisdom of these policies in the very process of deciding whether a particular state interest put forward may or may not be "compelling." The decision here to break pregnancy into three distinct terms and to outline the permissible restrictions the State may impose in each one, for example, partakes more of judicial legislation than it does of a determination of the intent of the drafters of the Fourteenth Amendment.

The fact that a majority of the States reflecting, after all, the majority sentiment in those States, have had restrictions on abortions for at least a century is a strong indication, it seems to me, that the asserted right to an abortion is not "so rooted in the traditions and conscience of our people as to be ranked as fundamental," *Snyder v. Massachusetts* (1934). Even today, when society's views on abortion are changing, the very existence of the debate is evidence that the "right" to an abortion is not so universally accepted as the appellant would have us believe.

To reach its result, the Court necessarily has had to find within the scope of the Fourteenth Amendment a right that was apparently completely unknown to the drafters of the

Amendment. As early as 1821, the first state law dealing directly with abortion was enacted by the Connecticut Legislature. By the time of the adoption of the Fourteenth Amendment in 1868, there were at least 36 laws enacted by state or territorial legislatures limiting abortion. While many States have amended or updated their laws, 21 of the laws on the books in 1868 remain in effect today. Indeed, the Texas statute struck down today was, as the majority notes, first enacted in 1857, and "has remained substantially unchanged to the present time."

There apparently was no question concerning the validity of this provision or of any of the other state statutes when the Fourteenth Amendment was adopted. The only conclusion possible from this history is that the drafters did not intend to have the Fourteenth Amendment withdraw from the States the power to legislate with respect to this matter.

## Respectful Dissent

Even if one were to agree that the case that the Court decides were here, and that the enunciation of the substantive constitutional law in the Court's opinion were proper, the actual disposition of the case by the Court is still difficult to justify. The Texas statute is struck down *in toto*, even though the Court apparently concedes that, at later periods of pregnancy Texas might impose these self-same statutory limitations on abortion. My understanding of past practice is that a statute found to be invalid as applied to a particular plaintiff, but not unconstitutional as a whole, is not simply "struck down" but is, instead, declared unconstitutional as applied to the fact situation before the Court.

For all of the foregoing reasons, I respectfully dissent.

# Student Suspension

## Byron White

*In the following Supreme Court opinion, the Court states that students suspended for disciplinary reasons have a right to notice of the charges against them and a hearing regarding their actions and punishments. In the opinion, Justice Byron White discusses the issue of public education and concludes that the Fourteenth Amendment's due process clause applies to student suspensions even though there is no constitutional right to a public education. White was appointed to the Supreme Court in 1962 by President John F. Kennedy and served until his retirement in 1993. He died in 2002.*

Mr. Justice White delivered the opinion of the Court.

This appeal by various administrators of the Columbus, Ohio, Public School System (CPSS) challenges the judgment of a three-judge federal court, declaring that appellees—various high school students in the CPSS—were denied due process of law contrary to the command of the Fourteenth Amendment in that they were temporarily suspended from their high schools without a hearing either prior to suspension or within a reasonable time thereafter, and enjoining the administrators to remove all references to such suspensions from the students' records.

Ohio law provides for free education to all children between the ages of six and 21. Section 3313.66 of the Code empowers the principal of an Ohio public school to suspend a pupil for misconduct for up to 10 days or to expel him. In either case, he must notify the student's parents within 24 hours and state the reasons for his action. A pupil who is expelled,

Byron White, *Goss et al v. Lopez et al*, U.S. Supreme Court, 419 U.S. 565, January 22, 1975. www.law.umkc.edu/faculty/projects/ftrials/conlaw/goss.html.

or his parents, may appeal the decision to the Board of Education and in connection therewith shall be permitted to be heard at the board meeting. The Board may reinstate the pupil following the hearing. No similar procedure is provided in § 3313.66 or any other provision of state law for a suspended student. Aside from a regulation tracking the statute, at the time of the imposition of the suspensions in this case the CPSS itself had not issued any written procedure applicable to suspensions. Nor, so far as the record reflects, had any of the individual high schools involved in this case. Each, however, had formally or informally described the conduct for which suspension could be imposed.

The nine named appellees, each of whom alleged that he or she had been suspended from public high school in Columbus for up to 10 days without a hearing pursuant to § 3313.66, filed an action under 42 U. S. C. § 1983 against the Columbus Board of Education and various administrators of the CPSS. The complaint sought a declaration that § 3313.66 was unconstitutional in that it permitted public school administrators to deprive plaintiffs of their rights to an education without a hearing of any kind, in violation of the procedural due process component of the Fourteenth Amendment. It also sought to enjoin the public school officials from issuing future suspensions pursuant to § 3313.66 and to require them to remove references to the past suspensions from the records of the students in question.

## Circumstances Surrounding the Suspensions

The proof below established that the suspensions arose out of a period of widespread student unrest in the CPSS during February and March 1971. Six of the named plaintiffs, Rudolph Sutton, Tyrone Washington, Susan Cooper, Deborah Fox, Clarence Byars, and Bruce Harris, were students at the Marion-Franklin High School and were each suspended for 10 days on account of disruptive or disobedient conduct committed in the presence of the school administrator who ordered the suspension. One of these, Tyrone Washington, was among a group of students demonstrating in the school auditorium while a class was being conducted there. He was ordered by the school principal to leave, refused to do so, and was suspended. Rudolph Sutton, in the presence of the principal, physically attacked a police officer who was attempting to remove Tyrone Washington from the auditorium. He was immediately suspended. The other four Marion-Franklin students were suspended for similar conduct. None was given a hearing to determine the operative facts underlying the suspension, but each, together with his or her parents, was offered the opportunity to attend a conference, subsequent to the effective date of the suspension, to discuss the student's future.

Two named plaintiffs, Dwight Lopez and Betty Crome, were students at the Central High School and McGuffey Junior High School, respectively. The former was suspended in connection with a disturbance in the lunchroom which involved some physical damage to school property. Lopez testified that at least 75 other students were suspended from his school on the same day. He also testified below that he was not a party to the destructive conduct but was instead an innocent bystander. Because no one from the school testified with regard to this incident, there is no evidence in the record indicating the official basis for concluding otherwise. Lopez never had a hearing.

Betty Crome was present at a demonstration at a high school other than the one she was attending. There she was arrested together with others, taken to the police station, and released without being formally charged. Before she went to school on the following day, she was notified that she had been suspended for a 10-day period. Because no one from the school testified with respect to this incident, the record does not disclose how the McGuffey Junior High School principal went about making the decision to suspend Crome, nor does it disclose on what information the decision was based. It is clear from the record that no hearing was ever held.

## Public Education Entitlement

At the outset, appellants contend that because there is no constitutional right to an education at public expense, the Due Process Clause does not protect against expulsions from the public school system. This position misconceives the nature of the issue and is refuted by prior decisions. The Fourteenth Amendment forbids the State to deprive any person of life, liberty, or property without due process of law. Protected interests in property are normally "not created by the Constitution. Rather, they are created and their dimensions are defined" by an independent source such as state statutes or rules entitling the citizen to certain benefits. Accordingly, a state employee who under state law, or rules promulgated by state officials, has a legitimate claim of entitlement to continued employment absent sufficient cause for discharge may demand the procedural protections of due process. So may welfare recipients who have statutory rights to welfare as long as they maintain the specified qualifications. *Morrissey v. Brewer* (1972) applied the limitations of the Due Process Clause to governmental decisions to revoke parole, although a parolee has no constitutional right to that status. Here, on the basis of state law, appellees plainly had legitimate claims of entitlement to a public education. Ohio Rev. Code Ann. §§ 3313.48 and 3313.64 direct local authorities to provide a free education to all residents between five and 21 years of age, and a compulsory-attendance law requires attendance for a school year of not less than 32 weeks. It is true that § 3313.66 of the Code permits school principals to suspend students for up to 10 days; but suspensions may not be imposed without any grounds whatsoever. All of the schools had their own rules specifying the grounds for expulsion or suspension. Having chosen to extend the right to an education to people of appellees' class generally, Ohio may not withdraw that right on grounds of misconduct, absent fundamentally fair procedures to determine whether the misconduct has occurred. Although Ohio may not be constitutionally obligated to establish and maintain a public school system, it has nevertheless done so and has required its children to attend. Those young people do not "shed their constitutional rights" at the schoolhouse door. "The Fourteenth Amendment, as now applied to the States, protects the citizen against the State itself and all of its creatures—Boards of Education not excepted." The authority possessed by the State to prescribe and enforce standards of conduct in its schools although concededly very broad, must be exercised consistently with constitutional safeguards.

## Other Aspects of Due Process

Among other things, the State is constrained to recognize a student's legitimate entitlement to a public education as a property interest which is protected by the Due Process Clause and which may not be taken away for misconduct without adherence to the minimum procedures required by that Clause. The Due Process Clause also forbids arbitrary deprivations of liberty. "Where a person's good name, reputation, honor, or integrity is at stake because of what the government is doing to him," the minimal requirements of the Clause must be satisfied. School authorities here suspended appellees from school for periods of up to 10 days based on charges of misconduct. If sustained and recorded, those charges could seriously damage the students' standing with their fellow pupils and their teachers as well as interfere with later opportunities for higher education and employment. It is apparent that the claimed right of the State to determine unilaterally and without process whether that misconduct has occurred immediately collides with the requirements of the Constitution.

Appellants proceed to argue that even if there is a right to a public education protected by the Due Process Clause generally, the Clause comes into play only when the State subjects a student to a "severe detriment or grievous loss." The loss of 10 days, it is said, is neither severe nor grievous and the Due Process Clause is therefore of no relevance. Appellants' argument is again refuted by our prior decisions; for in determining "whether due process requirements apply in the first place, we must look not to the 'weight' but to the *nature* of the interest at stake." Appellees were excluded from school only temporarily, it is true, but the length and consequent severity of a deprivation, while another factor to weigh in determining the appropriate form of hearing, "is not decisive of the basic right" to a hearing of some kind. A 10-day suspension from school is not *de minimis* [of minimum importance] in our view and may not be imposed in complete disregard of the Due Process Clause. A short suspension is, of course, a far milder deprivation than expulsion. But, "education is perhaps the most important function of state and local governments," and the total exclusion from the educational process for more than a trivial period, and certainly if the suspension is for 10 days, is a serious event in the life of the suspended child. Neither the property interest in educational benefits temporarily denied nor the liberty interest in reputation, which is also implicated, is so insubstantial that suspensions may constitutionally be imposed by any procedure the school chooses, no matter how arbitrary.

## What Process Is Due?

"Once it is determined that due process applies, the question remains what process is due." We turn to that question, fully realizing as our cases regularly do that the interpretation and application of the Due Process Clause are intensely practical matters and that "[the] very nature of due process negates any concept of inflexible procedures universally applicable to every imaginable situation." We are also mindful of our own admonition: "Judicial interposition in the operation of the public school system of the Nation raises problems requiring care and restraint. . . . By and large, public education in our Nation is committed to the control of state and local authorities." "The fundamental requisite of due process of law is the opportunity to be heard," a right that "has little reality or worth unless one is informed that the matter is pending and can choose for himself whether to . . . contest." At the very minimum, therefore, students facing suspension and the consequent interference with a protected property interest must be given *some* kind of notice and afforded *some* kind of hearing. "Parties whose rights are to be affected are entitled to be heard; and in order that they may enjoy that right they must first be notified." It also appears from our cases that the timing and content of the notice and the nature of the hearing will depend on appropriate accommodation of the competing interests involved. The student's interest is to avoid unfair or mistaken exclusion from the educational process, with all of its unfortunate consequences. The Due Process Clause will not shield him from suspensions properly imposed, but it disserves both his interest and the interest of the State if his suspension is in fact unwarranted. The concern would be mostly academic if the disciplinary process were a totally accurate, unerring process, never mistaken and never unfair. Unfortunately, that is not the case, and no one suggests that it is. Disciplinarians, although proceeding in utmost good faith, frequently act on the reports and advice of others; and the controlling facts and the nature of the conduct under challenge are often disputed. The risk of error is not at all trivial, and it should be guarded against if that may be done without prohibitive cost or interference with the educational process. The difficulty is that our schools are vast and complex. Some modicum of discipline and order is essential if the educational function is to be performed. Events calling for discipline are frequent occurrences and sometimes require immediate, effective action. Suspension is considered not only to be a necessary tool to maintain order but a valuable educational device. The prospect of imposing elaborate hearing requirements in every suspension case is viewed with great concern, and many school authorities may well prefer the untrammeled power to act unilaterally, unhampered by rules about notice and hearing. But it would be a strange disciplinary system in an educational institution if no communication was sought by the disciplinarian with the student in an effort to inform him of his dereliction and to let him tell his side of the story in order to make sure that an injustice is not done. "[Fairness] can rarely be obtained by secret, one-sided determination of facts decisive of rights. . . ." "Secrecy is not congenial to truth-seeking and self-righteousness gives too slender an assurance of rightness. No better instrument has been devised for arriving at truth than to give a person in jeopardy of serious loss notice of the case against him and opportunity to meet it."

## Notice Is Crucial

We do not believe that school authorities must be totally free from notice and hearing requirements if their schools are to operate with acceptable efficiency. Students facing temporary suspension have interests qualifying for protection of the Due Process Clause, and due process requires, in connection with a suspension of 10 days or less, that the student be given oral or written notice of the charges against him and, if he denies them, an explanation of the evidence the authorities have and an opportunity to present his side of the story. The Clause requires at least these rudimentary precautions against unfair or mistaken findings of misconduct and arbitrary exclusion from school.

There need be no delay between the time "notice" is given and the time of the hearing. In the great majority of cases the disciplinarian may informally discuss the alleged misconduct with the student minutes after it has occurred. We hold only that, in being given an opportunity to explain his version of the facts at this discussion, the student first be told what he is accused of doing and what the basis of the accusation is. Since the hearing may occur almost immediately following the misconduct, it follows that as a general rule notice and hearing should precede removal of the student from school. We agree with the District Court, however, that there are recurring situations in which prior notice and hearing cannot be insisted upon. Students whose presence poses a continuing danger to persons or property or an ongoing threat of disrupting the academic process may be immediately removed from school. In such cases, the necessary notice and rudimentary hearing should follow as soon as practicable, as the District Court indicated.

In holding as we do, we do not believe that we have imposed procedures on school disciplinarians which are inappropriate in a classroom setting. Instead we have imposed requirements which are, if anything, less than a fair-minded school principal would impose upon himself in order to avoid unfair suspensions.

## Longer Suspensions May Require More Formal Processes

We stop short of construing the Due Process Clause to require, countrywide, that hearings in connection with short suspensions must afford the student the opportunity to secure counsel, to confront and cross-examine witnesses supporting the charge, or to call his own witnesses to verify his version of the incident. Brief disciplinary suspensions are almost countless. To impose in each such case even truncated trial-type procedures might well overwhelm administrative facilities in many places and, by diverting resources, cost more than it would save in educational effectiveness. Moreover, further formalizing the suspension process and escalating its formality and adversary nature may not only make it too costly as a regular disciplinary tool but also destroy its effectiveness as part of the teaching process.

On the other hand, requiring effective notice and informal hearing permitting the student to give his version of the events will provide a meaningful hedge against erroneous action. At least the disciplinarian will be alerted to the existence of disputes about facts and arguments about cause and effect. He may then determine himself to summon the accuser, permit cross-examination, and allow the student to present his own witnesses. In more difficult cases, he may permit counsel. In any event, his discretion will be more informed and we think the risk of error substantially reduced.

We should also make it clear that we have addressed ourselves solely to the short suspension, not exceeding 10 days. Longer suspensions or expulsions for the remainder of the school term, or permanently, may require more formal procedures. Nor do we put aside the possibility that in unusual situations, although involving only a short suspension, something more than the rudimentary procedures will be required.

CONSTITUTIONAL
AMENDMENTS
BEYOND THE BILL OF RIGHTS

CHAPTER 3

# Current Due Process Issues

# Due Process and Detainees of the War on Terrorism

*Barbara Olshansky*

*As a result of the war on terrorism that began in response to the attacks of September 11, 2001, many individuals have been detained for various reasons. In the following selection Barbara Olshansky discusses the issues raised by detaining foreign nationals without due process. The Supreme Court has stated that due • process applies to all individuals within the United States. However, the Court has also upheld decisions that treat foreign na- − tionals differently than citizens. Olshansky discusses noncitizens' rights and the history behind those rights. She asserts that all persons in the United States are entitled to due process rights under the Fourteenth Amendment. Olshansky is former deputy legal director of the Center for Constitutional Rights and is a professor of human rights at Stanford University. She is the author of several books relating to civil and human rights and politics.*

The Bush administration's policies regarding foreign nationals raise several important issues. The first concerns the executive branch's willingness—and perhaps eagerness—to disregard established constitutional constraints, existing laws and regulations, and international law in order to allay what it perceives as the fears of the people and to implement the broadest-scale law enforcement initiative in order to do so. In the administration's furious rush to accomplish this end, the most fundamental guarantees against arbitrary executive action (like the well-established constitutional requirement of probable cause and the right to counsel in a criminal proceeding) fly out the window.

The government's steadily increasing trend toward unconstitutional action should be of great concern to us all. The ease with which the Justice Department—the FBI and the INS [Immigration and Naturalization Service]—dispensed with the constitutional requirement of due process when noncitizens' physical freedom was at stake is chilling. If the officials involved are not called to account for these deliberate constitutional and human rights violations, then we have truly become a country that disappears and imprisons people indefinitely without cause or justification.

Second, the fact that the government so easily chose to sacrifice the liberty of thousands of Arab, South Asian, and Muslim foreign nationals—particularly vulnerable minorities in this country—for the purported security of the rest of the country reveals a bias based on ignorance that pervades at the highest levels of government, as well as this country's deep ambivalence regarding the proper constitutional treatment of noncitizens. The category of Arab and Muslim countries whose citizens were selected for interrogation, registration, detention, and deportation made little sense given that several of those countries whose citizens were discriminatorily targeted, like Pakistan and Egypt, are now allies working with the United States in the "war on terror."

## The Supreme Court's Opinions Contradictory

The executive branch's ambivalence about who should be afforded the protection of the Constitution is well illustrated by our Supreme Court's decisions. On the one hand, the Supreme Court has held that the cardinal guarantee of the equal protection clause is "universal in its application, to all persons within the territorial jurisdiction, without regard to differences of . . . nationality" and that of the due process clause "applies to all 'persons' within the United States, including aliens, whether their presence here is lawful, unlawful, temporary, or permanent." The Court has further held that when

129

noncitizens are accused of crimes, they are entitled to all of the constitutional rights attaching to criminal trials: the right to a public trial, a trial by jury, the assistance of counsel, and the right to confront adverse witnesses. Constitutional scholars have noted that this view, which holds that foreign nationals are "persons" within the meaning of the Constitution, is premised in part on the notion that the Constitution itself only expressly reserves two rights for citizens, the right to vote and the right to run for federal elective office. This fact indicates that the Framers did not intend for the other constitutional rights to be exclusive to citizens.

On the other hand, at various points in its history, the Supreme Court has upheld the government's decisions to exclude and expel foreign nationals from the country because of their race; to bar them from owning land, even when the law provided only a thin veil for racism; to deport them for their political associations, even though those associations were not unlawful at the time; and to permit states to bar qualified foreign nationals from serving as public school teachers and police officers because of their immigration status.

## Noncitizens' Rights Are Important

Of these two polar positions, the extension of rights to noncitizens makes sense from several important perspectives. The system of legally enforceable constitutional rights balances the scales of liberty—the government's assertion of sovereignty over individuals has as its counterweight certain limitations on the exercise of governmental power. James Madison emphasized this compensating and counterbalancing function in his report condemning the Alien and Sedition Acts: "It does not follow, because aliens are not parties to the Constitution, as citizens are parties to it, that whilst they actually conform to it, they have no right to its protection. Aliens are no more parties to the laws than they are parties to the Constitution; yet it will not be disputed that, as they owe, on the one hand, a temporary obedience, they are entitled, in return, to their protection and advantage." The view espoused by James Madison that endures today is that those persons subject to the obligations of our laws ought to be able to invoke its protections as well.

Furthermore, the Madisonian view fully agrees with the contemporary human rights movement's understanding that there are equal and inalienable rights to which all persons are entitled, regardless of nationality, ethnicity, religion, immigration status, or political affiliation simply by virtue of their humanity. The Universal Declaration of Human Rights, the foundational document of international human rights discourse and practice, is based on the premise of "the inherent dignity and . . . the equal and inalienable rights of all members of the human family." The Universal Declaration guarantees the rights of due process, political expression and association, and equal protection and extends these rights to nationals and nonnationals alike. Other human rights covenants and treaties follow suit.

## Rights Are Owed to All

This country's "experiments" with diverting from the founding principle that fundamental rights are owed to all persons as a matter of human dignity provide a strong argument for acting in keeping with that legal and moral principle. The most frequently cited example is that of the decision in *Dred Scott v. Sandford*, in which the Court held that even African Americans freed from slavery could not avail themselves of the federal courts because they were "persons who are the descendants of Africans who were imported into this country, and sold as slaves"; they were "considered as a subordinate and inferior class of beings"; they were not protected by the Constitution when it was adopted, and therefore had no rights unless the government expressly chose to grant them. Congress expressly overruled this reasoning in the Civil Rights Act of 1866, and the Fourteenth Amendment made clear that all persons born or naturalized in the United States are citizens and that all persons present in the United States are entitled to due process of law and equal protection.

## Citizen Versus Noncitizen

Finally, constitutional scholars have raised the obvious question in this area and provided the most unassailable answer. Why should a country be able to take a noncitizen's life, liberty, or property without due process of law, when it cannot do the same to a citizen? People's interests in life and liberty do not vary depending on their nationality. Nor does the government's interest vary depending on citizenship status. The test used by the courts in determining how much process or constitutional protection is due to a person involves balancing the individual's interest with the government's interest, and the citizenship issue should not play any role in that assessment.

Unfortunately, neither our views as citizens nor the views of members of Congress were heard in this post September 11 debate. We were all not only locked out of the discussion about the immigration detention, registration, and deportation policies but were denied all information about its implementation. From the initial pronouncement by [U.S. attorney general John] Ashcroft that the Freedom of Information Act was suspended during the "war on terror," to the broad and unchecked dragnet cast over the Middle Eastern, South Asian, and Muslim immigrant communities—whose only identifiable connection to terrorism appeared to be the color of their skin, their religious affiliation, or the origin of their ancestors—to the hidden imprisonment of immigrants and the shameful "hold until cleared policy," to the secret deportation of people who seized, *the people of this country have been kept in the dark.*

ᵡ Under the banner of combating terrorism, Ashcroft authorized a pernicious assault on the protections guaranteed by the Fourth, Fifth, and Sixth Amendments to the Constitution. It was the Justice Department itself that impeded some of these most important rights and freedoms, including the right to personal liberty, the right to be free from unreasonable searches and seizures, the right to a speedy and public trial, and the right to individual privacy. Looking back on these actions now, who can say what we, *the People*, would have or could have done had we known of these wholesale constitutional and human rights violations?

# Music Piracy and the Right to Due Process

## Anita Ramasastry

*In the following selection Anita Ramasastry writes about the battle waged by the recording industry to stop music piracy via the Internet. To subpoena the offenders, the Recording Industry Association of America was using Internet protocol addresses without notifying the actual computer owners. Ramasastry argues that this practice violates the due process and privacy rights guaranteed by the Fourteenth Amendment. Also discussed are several court cases that deal with these due process issues. Ramasastry is a professor of law and a director of the Shidler Center for Law, Commerce, & Technology at the University of Washington School of Law in Seattle. She has written many articles on law, technology, and civil rights issues.*

Since 2003, the Recording Industry Association of America (RIAA) has been suing peer-to-peer (P2P) file swappers and downloaders. The RIAA alleges, in its suits, that P2P file swapping and downloading, when it involves pirated files, violates copyright law—and, at times, also the Digital Music Copyright Act (DMCA).

The RIAA's first set of suits—261 in all—was filed September 8, 2003. On September 30 of this year [2004], the RIAA filed 762 suits. This October, it filed 750 more. In total, the RIAA has filed more than 6,200 such suits.

## The Normal Subpoena Process

Here's how the RIAA typically proceeds. It files a "John Doe" lawsuit based on an Internet Protocol (IP) address connected to P2P trading via Kazaa, Grokster, Limewire, or another,

Anita Ramasastry, "Privacy, Piracy and Due Process in Peer-to-Peer File Swapping Suits: A Federal District Court Strikes a Good Balance," findlaw.com, November 10, 2004. Reproduced by permission. http://writ.news.findlaw.com.

---

## Schools with Individuals Cited for Music Piracy

*Over 200 colleges and universities have had individuals cited for music piracy, including:*

Arizona State University
Boston University
College of William and Mary
Columbia Univeristy
Drexel University
Indiana University
MIT
North Carolina State University
Ohio State University
Purdue University
Stanford University
Texas Christian University
Tufts University
University of Maine
University New Hampshire
University of Southern California
University of Utah
University of Virginia
University of Washington

The average cost for settling a music piracy claim is $3,000.

TAKEN FROM: Recording Industry Association of America.

---

similar system. The suit is often filed in the jurisdiction where the relevant Internet Service Provider (ISP) is located.

Once the suit is filed, the RIAA subpoenas the ISP to force it to disclose the real name of the "John Doe" associated with the IP address. That person, however, is not necessarily the file trader—it may instead be a relative, college roommate, or landlord. And neither that person—nor the file trader, if he or she is a different person—is given prior notice and a chance to fight the subpoena.

## Protecting Due Process

Fortunately, however, that may change. In late October, a U.S. District Court in Pennsylvania developed what I believe is a sensible and pragmatic approach to protect the Due Process and privacy rights of persons whose names are sought by of RIAA (and similar) subpoenas to their ISP[s].

The need to protect copyrighted works must be balanced against the need to protect constitutional rights. The district court's order strikes just such a balance.

## The *Elektra* Case: The Court Requires Notice to the John Doe Defendants

The Pennsylvania case is a civil copyright infringement action filed in March 2004, and entitled *Elektra Entertainment Group et al v. Does 1-6*. The plaintiffs, various record companies, subpoenaed the relevant ISP—the University of Pennsylvania ("Penn")—for the names of the six "John Doe" defendants—as well as, for each defendant, their address, telephone number, e-mail address, and Media Access Control address.

But the court held that before revealing the "John Does'" information, Penn must first alert the John Does; explain what has happen[ed]; and explain how they may contest the charges against them. The court also provided a model notice attached to its order for Penn to use—which included a resource list of attorneys and organizations assisting individuals whose ISPs have received this kind of subpoena.

(It turns out there are many such resources—such as the website of the Electronic Frontier Foundation. Indeed, there is even a specific Subpoenadefense.org website, which bills itself as a "resource for individuals seeking information on how to defend themselves if their identity has been subpoenaed by a private third party seeking to enforce their copyrights on the Internet," and also for individuals who have received RIAA subpoenas. But the subpoena targets—who, again, could easily have been the actual user's grandparents—are not necessarily aware of them.)

Finally, the court held that the John Does will remain anonymous for 21 days from the date of the notice—by which point, they must either file a motion to quash the plaintiff's subpoena to the ISP, or have their identities revealed. In addition, if they do file a motion to quash the subpoena, they will remain anonymous while the motion is pending.

## Prelude to *Elektra*: The D.C. Circuit's *Verizon* Decision

Even before the recent *Elektra* ruling, important—but partial—progress was made in honoring the constitutional rights of "John Does" in RIAA suits.

On December 19, 2003, in *RIAA v. Verizon Internet Services*, the U.S. Court of Appeals for the D.C. Circuit held that it was not sufficient for the RIAA to simply send an ISP a form subpoena demanding the identity of a particular Internet subscriber—as the RIAA had claimed was proper under the DMCA.

Rather, the court held, the RIAA had to first file a civil lawsuit against the "John Doe" defendants, and then seek a subpoena. The DMCA subpoena procedure, it ruled, only applied to materials hosted by an ISP—such as information stored on its servers—not materials for which the ISP merely acts as a conduit, such as P2P exchanges.

The *Elektra* decision builds on the *Verizon* decision by ensuring that the John Does have notice and an opportunity to contest the subpoenas to the ISPs, seeking their names. Previously, a customer's name would be disclosed before he or she even had a chance to challenge the subpoena to the ISP seeking the name.

## Protecting Anonymous Speech

Ultimately, the truly hard questions for courts will arise when they must confront the motions to quash the subpoenas to the ISPs. What *Elektra* wisely did was to ensure that "John Does" have a chance to file such motions. But it remains to be seen how the motions will be resolved.

Resolving some such motions will be simple—subpoenas may be quashed based on IP address mix-ups. But resolving the others may be very difficult.

On one hand, there are important First Amendment rights implicated by file swapping and other communications on the Internet. A fear that online speech is not truly anonymous could stifle multiple types of expression and investigation—many of them very valuable. (For instance, a teen abuse victim who is not ready to go to the police, might at least be ready to seek help anonymously in an online chatroom, or to search online for possible resources to help her.) Anonymity has encouraged candor throughout American history—even since the Founders used pseudonyms to communicate their views on the U.S. Constitution.

On the other hand, complete anonymity in cyberspace could allow Internet users to violate copyright laws with impunity. Worse, it could also make far worse crimes—such as terrorist acts—far easier.

The trick is to try to allow free speech to flourish, without making the Internet a safe harbor for terrorism. In the end, some balance is necessary.

That question isn't likely to go away anytime soon. But hopefully, the P2P question will someday.

With 60 million Americans using file-sharing software, despite the RIAA lawsuits, P2P sharing doesn't appear to be going away anytime soon. The record industry may do better talking to file sharers, than suing them. It is time for a truce.

# Due Process May Be Threatened by DNA Databases

*Marcelo Ballvé*

*DNA sampling is on the rise, according to the author of the following viewpoint. Many states are considering gathering DNA material from anyone arrested for a crime, and the U.S. government is hoping to expand the Federal Bureau of Investigation's DNA database. As Marcelo Ballvé reports, critics argue that this practice violates the idea that someone is innocent until proven guilty. It also threatens individuals' rights to due process and privacy. Ballvé is an editor and a writer.*

Genetics and crime fighting are becoming as intertwined as the DNA double helix. But that quickly evolving collaboration has taken a dangerous new twist.

Three states—Virginia, Louisiana and Texas—already require the collection of DNA samples from arrestees as part of the booking process, even before suspects go on trial. Critics see a worrying erosion of due process and what they call "DNA privacy"—the right of citizens to keep genetic information private.

## Collecting DNA

Nationwide, "DNA data-banking" policies vary, but over 30 states already require DNA collection from felons. California requires DNA sampling only from those convicted for violent felonies and some sex crimes.

But some want to go further, and take DNA samples from arrestees. Prop. 69, the "DNA Fingerprint" initiative, will be on November's [2004] ballot and already enjoys broad bipartisan support. If voters pass it, California—a bellwether state for criminal justice trends—will have among the country's most sweeping DNA sampling policies.

Proposition 69 already has momentum. On July 7, Republican Gov. Arnold Schwarzenegger announced his support. Attorney General Bill Lockyer, a Democrat, also backs it.

If approved, DNA collection would go into effect immediately for suspects arrested for murder or rape. They would have their DNA sampled by mouth swabs as part of the booking process. Beginning in 2009, samples would be taken from individuals arrested for a felony crime in California.

Critics say this is a blatant violation of the principle that one is innocent until proven guilty. Although arrestees who are not convicted can later have their DNA removed from databases, this would involve a bureaucratic process.

The Bush administration is keen on expanding the FBI's DNA database, known as CODIS, which pools together state databases. Under current law, only the DNA profiles of convicts can be placed in the federal database. Last year, U.S Justice Department officials spoke with members of Congress wanting them to lift that restriction so that the DNA of some arrestees, including juveniles, can also be made available through the database.

## Very Personal Information

Advocates of "DNA Fingerprinting" claim that even if innocent people are sometimes forced to give DNA, the practice is no more risky than the traditional ink or digitally scanned fingerprint that people nowadays submit to routinely. They also say that only a portion of the DNA sample submitted is actually uploaded to the database.

Opponents reply that law enforcement still holds the entire sample. Unlike a fingerprint, that puts the most intimate information that an individual possesses at the government's disposal.

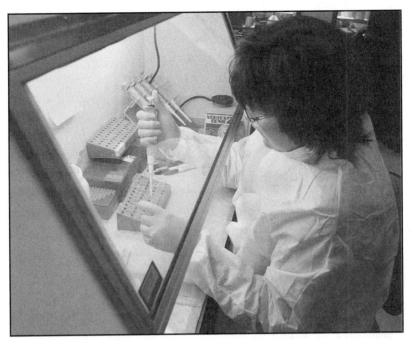

*Forensic scientists use DNA testing to assist in the identification of an individual based on the basis of their respective DNA profiles.* AP Images.

"Fingerprints . . . are useful only as a form of identification," Barry Steinhardt of the American Civil Liberties Union told the National Commission on the Future of DNA Evidence. "The DNA samples that are being held by state and local governments can provide insights into the most personal family relationships and the most intimate workings of the human body."

## Database Expansion

Police DNA databases have expanded rapidly. In 2003 alone, over a dozen states changed their laws to expand the scope of their DNA collection. When first proposed, most plans called for the compulsory sampling of convicted sex offenders. Today, three states take DNA from arrestees and similar plans are showing up on ballots and rattling around in state capitals nationwide.

Since a bigger database increases the possibility of a match with genetic material from a crime scene, law enforcement hunger for DNA continues to grow—even going beyond arrestees.

One major fear is law enforcement will begin using genetic evidence to create a 21st century version of racial profiling. Already, police in Charlottesville, Va., had to face accusations that they were casting a "DNA dragnet," aggressively collecting saliva samples from African Americans in a serial rape case.

Bruce Harrington, the California proposition's sponsor, has deeply personal reasons for seeking a large DNA database. A serial rapist and murderer killed his sister and brother-in-law in 1980 in a case that remains unsolved.

But as the entire nation witnessed during the trial of O.J. Simpson, strong DNA evidence is no sure-fire legal tool. Genetic evidence does not "prove" innocence or guilt. Supposedly infallible DNA evidence is subject to human error through mishandling, contamination and misinterpretation. A skillful lawyer can shatter a case built on a DNA "match."

## The Right to Informed Consent

The Council for Responsible Genetics, a Cambridge, Mass.–based nonprofit, issued a proposed "Genetic Bill of Rights" in 2000. Article 7 says all people should be able to prevent the taking or storing of bodily samples for genetic information without their voluntary informed consent.

In proposals like Proposition 69, U.S. society is setting precedents for how highly this right will be valued, or if it will be respected at all. The problem is not the use of DNA in courtrooms, in legal actions to exonerate the innocent or as a part of police work. Those uses already are common, often with the consent of those submitting DNA. The issue is who will be forced to give up their genetic information. If arrestees have the right to remain silent, shouldn't they also have the right to keep their DNA to themselves?

# Immigration Reform Could Threaten Due Process Rights

*American Civil Liberties Union*

*In this viewpoint the American Civil Liberties Union (ACLU) contends that immigration law reform needs to address better protection of due process rights. According to the ACLU, one of the ideas under consideration is an employment eligibility program that would violate privacy rights and cost businesses both money and time. Also discussed is the issue of directing all immigration litigation through the U.S. Court of Appeals for the Federal Circuit. According to the ACLU, this practice would overwhelm the court system and deny individuals the full benefits of the right to due process. The ACLU is an organization focused on individual rights and liberties.*

As legislation to reform the nation's immigration laws stalled in the Senate today [April 2006], the American Civil Liberties Union urged lawmakers to modify that legislation to better protect privacy, judicial review and due process rights.

"Immigration reform should not become the means to undermine the Constitution, nor should it place undue burdens on the American worker," said Caroline Fredrickson, Director of the ACLU Washington Legislative Office. "Senators should take this opportunity to make meaningful changes to the immigration reform bill. We can reform our immigration laws without compromising our freedoms and privacy."

While the Senate has been unable to come to an agreement on specific legislation, the ACLU noted that the compet-

*A man calls for immigration reform at a protest. The Comprehensive Immigration Reform Act of 2007 was a bill that would have provided legal status and a path to legal citizenship for the approximately 12 million illegal immigrants currently residing in the United States. AP Images.*

ing bills recognize that "enforcement-only" approaches to immigration reform do not work. However, some proposals would expand deeply flawed policies that have already eroded due process and civil liberties and should be jettisoned or overhauled.

## Government Permission to Work

One major point of contention is the lack of privacy protections in the proposed Employment Verification System. This proposal would require—for the first time—*all* workers to obtain a federal agency's permission to work, regardless of citi-

145

zenship or immigration status. All employers would be required to participate in a national employment eligibility verification program in an expansion of the faulty but voluntary "Basic Pilot" program.

The new program would likely use an Internet-based system to check the names and Social Security numbers of all employees—citizens and non-citizen[s] alike—against two government agencies' databases. But, legislators have not provided for a secure system. Thus, the data provides a ripe target for identity thieves.

This move would also place a huge burden on both employers and workers. The non-partisan Government Accountability Office [GAO] found that conservative estimates of implementation costs are at least $11.7 billion annually, a large share of which would be borne by businesses. Also, even assuming a near-perfect accuracy rate, millions of legal, eligible American workers could still have their right to work seriously delayed or denied—while they fight bureaucratic red tape to resolve errors. The conservative Heritage Foundation, the U.S. Chamber of Commerce and other business organizations have expressed strong objections to the employment verification provisions.

## New "Hard Cards"

Some have also called for the "hardening" of Social Security Cards to make them tamper-proof. Recent GAO reports estimate that issuing such a card to all Americans and lawful permanent residents would cost at least $9 billion and it would take 67,000 work *years*. The commissioner of the Social Security Administration recently said it would take a doubling of her existing staff of more than 60,000 people to implement. The ACLU noted that technological glitches, database errors and bureaucratic bungling would also be inevitable.

# Inexperienced and Overwhelmed Courts

The Senate also unwisely proposes to direct all immigration appeals to one court: the U.S. Court of Appeals for the Federal Circuit. Congress has yet to fully consider this radical proposal, which would undermine the rights of immigrants to judicial review. Furthermore, the Federal Circuit Court of Appeals has no experience with immigration, civil rights, or related constitutional claims—claims that could overwhelm the court.

Another provision would institute one-judge pre-screening of cases that get to the federal circuit court level. Under this provision, if the judge does not act on a case within 60 days, the case gets dismissed. If the judge *does* find the case meritorious, that judge would then issue a "certificate of reviewability" that allows the case to be heard by a three-judge panel.

The ACLU noted that given the high workloads faced by America's federal courts, it is all too likely that many immigrants' appeals would never receive serious review from a judge and would be dismissed without any judicial consideration of their merits.

# No Day in Court

"With this complex issue, the devil is truly in the details," said Timothy Sparapani, ACLU Legislative Counsel. "Too much of the debate has not been focused on provisions that would bar the courthouse door for many immigrants who deserve their day in court and would require that *everyone* in the United States who wants to work must apply for 'permission to work' from the government. Congress should not pass a bill until these misdirected provisions are addressed."

# Appendices

# Appendix A

## The Amendments to the U.S. Constitution

Amendment I:    Freedom of Religion, Speech, Press, Petition, and Assembly (ratified 1791)

Amendment II:    Right to Bear Arms (ratified 1791)

Amendment III:    Quartering of Soldiers (ratified 1791)

Amendment IV:    Freedom from Unfair Search and Seizures (ratified 1791)

Amendment V:    Right to Due Process (ratified 1791)

Amendment VI:    Rights of the Accused (ratified 1791)

Amendment VII:    Right to Trial by Jury (ratified 1791)

Amendment VIII:    Freedom from Cruel and Unusual Punishment (ratified 1791)

Amendment IX:    Construction of the Constitution (ratified 1791)

Amendment X:    Powers of the States and People (ratified 1791)

Amendment XI:    Judicial Limits (ratified 1795)

Amendment XII:    Presidential Election Process (ratified 1804)

Amendment XIII:    Abolishing Slavery (ratified 1865)

Amendment XIV:    Equal Protection, Due Process, Citizenship for All (ratified 1868)

# The Amendments to the U.S. Constitution

Amendment XV:      Race and the Right to Vote (ratified 1870)
Amendment XVI:     Allowing Federal Income Tax (ratified 1913)
Amendment XVII:    Establishing Election to the U.S. Senate
                   (ratified 1913)
Amendment XVIII:   Prohibition (ratified 1919)
Amendment XIX:     Granting Women the Right to Vote (ratified 1920)
Amendment XX:      Establishing Term Commencement for Congress
                   and the President (ratified 1933)
Amendment XXI:     Repeal of Prohibition (ratified 1933)
Amendment XXII:    Establishing Term Limits for U.S. President
                   (ratified 1951)
Amendment XXIII:   Allowing Washington, D.C., Representation in the
                   Electoral College (ratified 1961)
Amendment XXIV:    Prohibition of the Poll Tax (ratified 1964)
Amendment XXV:     Presidential Disability and Succession
                   (ratified 1967)
Amendment XXVI:    Lowering the Voting Age (ratified 1971)
Amendment XXVII:   Limiting Congressional Pay Increases
                   (ratified 1992)

# Appendix B

## Court Cases Relevant to the Fourteenth Amendment's Due Process Clause

### *United States v. Cruikshank,* 1876

This case before the Supreme Court involved a group of white men accused of violating the civil rights of blacks. In a unanimous decision, the Court said that the Fourteenth Amendment did not protect one citizen from the actions of another citizen.

### *Civil Rights Cases,* 1883

Several black civil rights cases were brought to the Supreme Court and heard under one heading. The Court ruled that Congress did not have the power to protect individuals from private discrimination and that the protection afforded by the Fourteenth Amendment applied only to actions by the states themselves.

### *Mugler v. Kansas,* 1887

Peter Mugler was arrested for making beer without a state license. He argued that the police did not have the right to prohibit his making beer for private consumption or sale outside of Kansas and that the law deprived him of property without due process. The Supreme Court upheld the state statute, but the dissenting opinion argued that taking the beer violated the due process clause of the Fourteenth Amendment.

### *Chicago, Milwaukee & St. Paul Ry. Co. v. Minnesota,* 1890

In this case the Supreme Court ruled that judicial review was required of a railroad's rate-making practices. It was one of the first Supreme Court cases to apply substantive due process.

### Chicago, Burlington & Quincy Railroad Co. v. Chicago, 1897

The Supreme Court ruled that states have to award just compensation when taking private property for public use because there is no due process of law if there is no just compensation. This case was one of the first instances of the Court using due process to protect substantive private-property rights.

### Holden v. Hardy, 1898

The Supreme Court upheld a Utah law setting an eight-hour workday for miners. The state court had ruled that working more than eight hours in mining tunnels posed a threat to the workers. The mining company had argued that due process gave it the right to negotiate whatever contract it wanted with its workers.

### Lochner v. New York, 1905

In this federal case the Supreme Court ruled against a New York state law that determined maximum working hours for bakers as sixty hours per week or ten hours per day. The bakery owner Joseph Lochner claimed that limiting his hours violated his right to life, liberty, or property without due process. The court stated that due process granted the business owner the right to make a living and that set working hours would interfere with that right.

### Gitlow v. New York, 1925

In this case the Supreme Court changed direction on its view regarding the personal liberties of citizens. Justice Edward Sanford stated, "We may and do assume that freedom of speech and of the press—which are protected by the First Amendment from abridgement by Congress—are among the fundamental personal rights and 'liberties' protected by the due process clause of the Fourteenth Amendment from impairment by the States."

### Morehead v. New York ex rel. Tipaldo, 1936
The Supreme Court narrowly struck down a minimum-wage law for women and children. The Court once again decided that the right to contract freely for wages was protected by the Constitution.

### West Coast Hotel v. Parrish, 1937
The Supreme Court changed its opinion on minimum wage by upholding a Washington state minimum-wage law for women. This issue was almost identical to the previous year's *Morehead v. Tipaldo* case, but the Court stated that the company's liberty, while protected by the Constitution, could still be restrained by government regulation, because such regulation protects the due process rights of the community.

### Mapp v. Ohio, 1961
The Supreme Court used this case to state that the Fourth Amendment right to privacy is made enforceable at a state level by the Fourteenth Amendment's due process clause.

### Gideon v. Wainwright, 1963
When Clarence Gideon was first convicted of burglary in 1961, he was not allowed the services of a court-appointed defense attorney and had to represent himself. After his conviction Gideon wrote a letter to the Supreme Court, asking the justices to hear his case. They accepted and ruled that all felony defendants were entitled to legal counsel. Gideon had his case tried again, with a lawyer, and was found not guilty on all charges.

### Griswold v. Connecticut, 1965
This case before the Supreme Court dealt with contraception use by married couples. A Connecticut law made it illegal for married couples to use contraception, and this law was challenged on the grounds that it infringed on an individual's personal liberty guaranteed under the due process clause of the Fourteenth Amendment. The law was ruled unconstitutional

because it infringed on a married couple's right to privacy. The Court ended up with four differing justifications for their decision.

### *Schmerber v. California,* 1966

In this Supreme Court case involving the extent of police power and due process, the Court stated that police had the authority to test the defendant for blood-alcohol levels without treading on his due process rights. The Court also stated, "That we today hold that the Constitution does not forbid the States minor intrusions into an individual's body under stringently limited conditions in no way indicates that it permits more substantial intrusions, or intrusions under other conditions."

### *In Re Gault,* 1967

In this landmark juvenile court case, the Supreme Court ruled that notice must be given in accordance with due process requirements in the cases of juvenile court hearings and proceedings. Before this case no notice was legally necessary when dealing with children.

### *Stanley v. Georgia,* 1969

The Supreme Court used this case to define the right of personal privacy as guaranteed by the due process clause of the Fourteenth Amendment. Justice Thurgood Marshall wrote in the opinion, "For also fundamental is the right to be free, except in very limited circumstances, from unwanted governmental intrusions into one's privacy."

### *Roe v. Wade,* 1973

The Supreme Court decided that the right of privacy, guaranteed by due process, gave women the right to an abortion, striking down state laws that said otherwise. The dissenting opinion stated that the due process clause placed limits on the right to abortion.

## Goss et al. v. Lopez et al., 1975

In this case regarding juvenile rights, the Supreme Court ruled that students have the right to a hearing regarding disciplinary actions when faced with a short-term suspension of not more than ten days.

## Planned Parenthood of Southeastern Pennsylvania v. Casey, 1992

In this abortion case, the Supreme Court, in a 5–4 split, decided to uphold *Roe v. Wade* but allowed for states to place restrictions on abortions. The Court nevertheless stated that those limits could not cause an "undue burden."

## Rasul v. Bush, 2004

In this case the Supreme Court ruled that foreigners detained at the U.S. facilities in Guantanamo Bay, Cuba, on suspicion of terrorism would be granted access to the U.S. Federal Court system to challenge their detention.

## Hamdi v. Rumsfeld, 2004

In this second case involving detainees suspected of terrorism, Yaser Hamdi, a U.S. citizen, was captured in Afghanistan and sent to Cuba. When it was discovered that he was a citizen, he was shipped to the United States for detention. The U.S. government wished to treat Hamdi as an enemy combatant without any of the constitutional rights available to citizens. The Supreme Court ruled that Hamdi should have the means to present evidence in his defense.

## Munaf v. Geren, 2008

In this case, heard by the Supreme Court in March 2008, the justices were asked again to decide if detainees held by U.S. authorities have the right to appear before a U.S. court, even if the individual is being held outside the United States. The Court ruled that U.S. citizens held overseas by the U.S. military have a right to appear in U.S. courts.

# For Further Research

## Books

David J. Bodenhamer, *Fair Trial: Rights of the Accused in American History*. New York: Oxford University Press, 1992.

James E. Bond, *No Easy Walk to Freedom: Reconstruction and the Ratification of the Fourteenth Amendment*. Westport, CT: Praeger Publishers, 1997.

Michael Kent Curtis, *No State Shall Abridge: The Fourteenth Amendment and the Bill of Rights*. Durham, NC: Duke University Press, 1986.

Joseph B. James, *The Ratification of the Fourteenth Amendment*. Macon, GA: Mercer University Press, 1984.

Mark R. Levin, *Men in Black: How the Supreme Court Is Destroying America*. Washington, DC: Regnery Publishing, 2005.

Jane Meyer, *The Dark Side: The Inside Story of How the War on Terror Turned into a War on American Ideals*. New York: Doubleday, 2008.

William E. Nelson, *The Fourteenth Amendment: From Political Principal to Judicial Doctrine*. Cambridge, MA: Harvard University Press, 1988.

John V. Orth, *Due Process of Law: A Brief History*. Lawrence: University Press of Kansas, 2003.

Michael J. Perry, *We the People: The Fourteenth Amendment and the Supreme Court*. New York: Oxford University Press, 1999.

Richard Stiller, *Broken Promises: The Strange History of the Fourteenth Amendment*. New York: Random House, 1972.

## Periodicals

Keith R. Denny, "That Old Due Process Magic: Growth Control and the Federal Constitution," *Michigan Law Review*, vol. 88, no. 5, 1990.

Justin Ewers, "Journey into a Dark Past," *US News & World Report*, May 19, 2008.

Linda Greenhouse, "Justices Uphold Taking Property for Development," *New York Times*, June 24, 2005.

Jonathan Mahler, "Enemy Number One," *Time*, August 4, 2008.

David G. Savage, "High Court Debates Rights of Guantanamo Detainees," *Los Angeles Times*, December 6, 2007.

Emma Schwartz, "A Chance for Justice at Last," *US News & World Report*, February 25/March 3, 2008.

———, "Cracking Down on Border Crossers," *US News & World Report*, April 18, 2008.

*Washington Post*, "Jose Padilla's Due Process," August 17, 2007.

## Internet Sources

Amy Goldstein, "Critics Say Bill Dimishes Due Process for Immigrants," *Washington Post*, May 26, 2006. www.washingtonpost.com.

Lino A. Graglia, "Rule of Law: Our Constitution Faces Death by 'Due Process,'" *Wall Street Journal*, May 24, 2005. www.opinionjournal.com.

Tom Malinowski, "Testimony on Improving Detainee Policy: Handling Terrorism Detainees Within the American Justice System," *Human Rights News*, June 4, 2008. http://hrw.org.

Jenny S. Martinez, "Process and Substance in the 'War on Terror,'" *Columbia Law Review*, vol. 108, no. 5, June 2008. www.columbialawreview.org.

Thomas F. Powers, "Due Process for Terrorists?" *Weekly Standard*, January 12, 2004. www.weeklystandard.com.

Warren Richey, "At Court, A Terror Case Rife with Tough Issues," *Christian Science Monitor*, March 27, 2006. www.csmonitor.com.

Jeffrey Rosen, "A Terror Trial, With or Without Due Process," *New York Times*, September 10, 2006. www.nytimes.com.

Emma Schwartz, "Supreme Court Hears a Key Case on Detainee Rights," *US News & World Report*, March 24, 2008. www.usnews.com.

## Web Sites

**HarpWeek Explore History**, http://14thamendment. harpweek.com. This site, subtitled "Citizenship, Due Process, and Equal Protection: The Creation of the Fourteenth Amendment," offers information about the creation of the history of the Fourteenth Amendment. Site features include a detailed time line, in-depth commentaries, biographies of key individuals, and a glossary of relevant terms.

**U.S. Constitution Online**, www.usconstitution.net. This site provides the complete wording of the U.S. Constitution along with a glossary and a list of thirty-five topics, including due process, military justice, and separation of powers. Also included is a list of related topics, such as events affecting the Constitution, the framers of the Constitution, and the Constitution for kids.

**U.S. Supreme Court Center, Fourteenth Amendment**, http:// supreme.justia.com. This site offers in-depth information on many aspects of due process, including labor, business enterprise, public utilities, state resources, taxation, eminent domain, and others.

# Index